D0104862

THE LAW SCHOOL ADMISSION GAME
PLAY LIKE AN EXPERT

ANN K. LEVINE, ESQ.

A LAW SCHOOL EXPERT PUBLICATION OF
ABRAHAM PUBLISHING, INC.
SANTA BARBARA, CA

Library of Congress Catalog Number: 2009902394
ISBN: 978-0-615-27183-5
Published by Abraham Publishing, Inc., Santa Barbara, CA
Printed on recycled paper in the United States of America.

THE LAW SCHOOL
ADMISSION GAME

CONTENTS

ACKNOWLEDGEMENTS

I gratefully acknowledge:

My previous professional mentors:

Cindy Rold, for training me to be a perfectionist when it didn't come naturally.

Professor Phil Manns, for giving me the chance to be a 26 year-old law school Director of Admissions.

Gary Hill, for firing me and thereby forcing me to make the second best decision I ever made, which was starting lawschoolexpert.com.

Those who worked with me to make Law School Expert *an overwhelming success during its first five years:*

Brent, for believing in me and in this business, for giving me the confidence to be an entrepreneur, and serving as my "de-facto" business manager while giving me the freedom to trust my own judgment. Marrying him is the absolute best decision I ever made.

Lorrie Thomas, Kate McMillan & the Wild Web Women for understanding my vision and giving me the tools to make it happen.

Felisa Manion, for taking on the grunt work happily and keeping me from drowning.

Those who support and inspire me:

My parents, Stephen and Janis Kowel, for passing along high standards for the things that matter and for cultivating my independence.

Brent's parents, Robert and Susan Levine, for their unconditional support and confidence in my abilities.

To our siblings, Gene Kowel, Rose Kowel Durbin, Matt Durbin, and Erin Levine, for being incredibly accomplished and committed to their work and serving as continual inspiration.

The clients, friends, and colleagues, who took the time to provide me with feedback on this book, include:

Ebby Abraham, Christina Ahn, Marisa Agha (who came up with the title), Linda Ashar, Stuart Baimel, Randee Breiter, Sarah Oulton, Ethan Park, Charles Roboski, Bara Sapir, Steve Schwartz, Greg Shaffer, Rebecca Sivitz, Sara Yood, and Joy Zeigeweid.

DEDICATION

For Haley and Nicole:
Dream Big. Do Good. Be True.

INTRODUCTION

THE decision to attend law school is a big one. It's expensive, time consuming, and it will take effort and initiative to see results from your labors and investment. If you are reading this book, you are seriously considering applying to law school. People have many reasons for applying:

- Personal experience with the legal system – whether through a parental divorce, a legal assistant position, an internship, or witnessing how the law impacts daily life in some other way.
- A general desire to find a profession that provides financial security and prestige.
- Coursework in a field that encouraged critical thinking and enjoyment of the processes and issues.
- Enthusiasm for social justice, civil rights, and public interest.
- General interest in intellectual development and progressing in a career.

My husband came up with a name for a syndrome I witness repeatedly from the law school applicants who comment on my blog, email me, and work with me as a law school admission consultant. He calls it "Application Panic Syndrome."

"Application Panic Syndrome" appears to have many specific and cumulative causes, including:

1. Being overwhelmed by the vast amount of information available to law school applicants from sources including commercial enterprises, supposedly helpful parents and friends, the Internet, and the law schools themselves who may not have your best interests at heart;

2. Trying to understand LSDAS, LSAC and the LSAT, U.S. News, LSN, LSD, TLS, LORs, AdCom, and many other acronyms;

3. Fretting over that minor-in-possession ticket from when you were 19, worrying you'll never get into law school as a result, and stressing over how to explain this to law schools intelligently and productively;

4. Deciding how to prepare for the LSAT, which prep course to take, deciding whether to cancel the LSAT, waiting for your LSAT score, deciding whether to retake the LSAT, and wondering whether your LSAT score will be good enough for any of the schools on your list;

5. Trying to come up with the most brilliant and effective law school personal statement ever written when you have not solved strife in the Middle East while overcoming paralysis and personally orchestrating the election of President Obama.

6. Wondering what it really means when a school sends you an email with a fee waiver, no strings attached;

7. Reading Law School Discussion and Top-Law-Schools or other online forums and seeing that (a) some

people have already applied to law school, (b) some people may have already been admitted to law schools, and (c) those people are really enjoying their bragging rights (they are probably the same people who will be known as "jerks" in your section next fall);

8. Wondering why UVA hasn't called you for an interview while the other person with the 3.9 and 168 got an interview, and why your friend with lower numbers got the scholarship to Cardozo while your application is "on hold."

These are the kinds of issues that I help my clients resolve. Since opening Law School Expert in 2004, I have helped tens of thousands of law school applicants through private admission consulting and by providing advice on the Law School Expert blog. After five years of running Law School Expert, I decided to write this book because:

- As Director of Admissions for two ABA law schools, I witnessed applicants make material mistakes on applications. I read personal statements that gave me more reasons to reject applicants than accept them, and met applicants to my law school whose interactions with me and with members of my staff caused me to put them in the "no way" pile before I even read their applications.

- The one-on-one nature of the services I provide as a law school admission consultant prohibits me from working individually with more than 200 applicants each year. Yet, the 100,000 people who read my blog last year seem to have the same questions and concerns, many of which are impossible to answer in a blog format.

- You will benefit from having a year-round resource at your disposal that you can thumb through whenever you think of a question about the law school admission process. At first, you may want to know how and why to register for LSDAS, and later on you will want to know what you can do if you are waitlisted. This book is for those moments, and every other moment, of this anxiety-inducing process.

Many readers of my blog have told me that I served as the calm voice of reason in the moments when they most needed perspective. I hope this book will do the same and will help you through the times when you find yourself suffering from Application Panic Syndrome.

A note about my perspective:

Most advice is subjective by its very nature. It's important to know who the advice is coming from and what that person's experiences are in order to put the suggestions in context and know whether to trust the advice. When reading this book, please keep in mind that my experience as director of admissions for two ABA law schools and director of student services for a third means that I was trained to see things as the law schools see things. I know what's been seen a thousand times, and I know how law schools, particularly those fickle faculty members, will respond to certain information on applications. Therefore:

- My bias is in favor of being candid and ethical in all dealings with law schools.
- I will be quite candid about the role of underrepresented minority (URM) status in the application process. My comments are not representative of my personal beliefs or political leanings on whether the results are right or wrong; they are simply offered as a dose of realism for law school applicants.
- I am a big believer in taking advantage of the rolling admission process, and all of my advice is slanted in this respect because I believe it offers applicants the greatest opportunities for success.
- I believe in the value of a "Fourth Tier" or "Regional Law School" education for the right person. I am not a school snob. Top law schools are great for some candidates, and regional law schools are great for other candidates.
- I feel strongly that law school applicants must understand that jobs are not handed out along with diplomas for most law school graduates. You must expect to hustle, work hard, and build your own bridges to your career goals.
- I will make blunt comments on occasion, so if you are used to your parents solving your problems, editing your papers, and telling you that their best friend from the country club will write your letter of recommendation to Georgetown, please prepare to be caught off guard by some of the realities I present.
- My bias is against discussion forums and advice given anonymously by people with no direct experience making law school admission decisions. One of

my clients who currently attends the University of California Davis School of Law (King Hall) said it best. "These forums are full of people who are trying to psych each other out (kind of like law school)! I think the forums are well-intentioned but poorly executed, and, thus, so toxic!"

- I am not an LSAT tutor. Although I have expertise in how the law schools interpret scores, I included references to experts on LSAT preparation when I believed it would be helpful to those reading this book.

- I do not consider it my job to convince anyone whether law school is the right decision. You must do your own research into the profession and think about your goals and aspirations. I do not create the dream of attending law school; I help you attain it. It's a decision you should not take lightly.

How to use this book:

It is impossible to account for every possible situation and applicant in the confines of a book. I also believe advice books can only help those who are open to help. If you're certain a piece of advice doesn't apply to your situation because you present an unwritten exception to a rule, you will not benefit from the advice given.

Throughout this book, you will see comments and advice from colleagues, attorneys, and former clients. These comments are intended to shed additional light on the relevant topics from the perspective of the applicant and law student.

This book is organized to introduce you to the major components of the admission process. It has three sections:

Part I: Getting Started

> This section provides an introduction to the law
> school admission process, including planning details
> for those applying more than one year in the future.

Part II: Applying to Law School

> This section emphasizes the application and deciding
> where to apply.

Part III: Making a Decision

> The final section provides food for thought about
> important considerations in choosing a law school
> and things to remember upon entering the legal
> profession.

PART I

GETTING STARTED

CHAPTER 1

LOOKING AHEAD

Advice for People Who Are Going to Apply to
Law School More Than One Year From Now

MOST of this book is geared toward people who will be applying to law school in the next 1-18 months. However, there are things you can do while still in college to strengthen your eventual applications. The following advice applies to those of you who are more than a year away from applying to law school.

PICKING A MAJOR

Those of you still in college may be wondering how your choice of major comes into play. Those of you for whom this decision is already made might be wondering how your undergraduate major will stack up against others'. Here is a rundown of the major groupings and how law schools are apt to evaluate you based on your undergraduate major area of study:

1. **Science Majors:** You often risk having a lower GPA, but it can be excused because of the difficult curriculum and lab hours. Of course, it also helps to make the case that you want to be a patent/IP lawyer if you have a science/math background. However, it can also

risk looking like you really would have preferred to go to med school but you just didn't have the GPA. You will find that law schools like it if you did well in a science major, and it will help you in the admissions process. For those of you worried that your physics degree will be competing against history degrees, I would say that if your grades are solid, you have strong academic letters, and perhaps someone who can attest to your writing ability, you'll find yourself at no inherent disadvantage in the admission process and you may even stand out.

2. **Pre-Law Majors:** Law and Society, Pre-Law, Political Science, and Criminal Justice studies show you have a sincere interest in the subject matter. It's especially helpful if you do a thesis and significant academic or internship work to supplement the curriculum. However, lackluster grades in these subjects will not impress an admission office. A 3.3 GPA in political science is not the same as a 3.3 in biomedical engineering or physics, and law schools will not fill classes with 100 political science majors. Diversity counts.

3. **Communication and Education Majors:** If you have not achieved a very solid GPA, be aware that many law school admission committees tend to view these majors as being less demanding. "Committees have been known to 'discount' these majors by as much as .5, meaning that a 3.25 in criminal justice might be equated with a 3.0 in political science or a 2.75 in the sciences," according to Charles Roboski, Assistant Dean of Admission and Financial Aid at Michigan State University College of Law.

4. **Art and Music Majors**: A BFA makes things tricky, but if you do well academically and do a thesis or have something to show for yourself other than being an unemployed actor, this absolutely works. Actually, Art History is one of the best majors for preparing you for law school because it teaches you to look at something you've never seen before and apply the facts you've learned to determine what you're looking at. That's pretty much a law school exam in a nutshell. Anything that shows you've done some serious writing will help. Music composition shows you're a thinking person. If your theatre program included significant reading and analysis, have a professor emphasize this in a Letter of Recommendation (LOR) to help explain the value of your course of study.

5. **Business Majors**: A major in marketing is not so impressive, but if you have strong grades and showed a sincere interest in serious things, it's fine. Economics is better because it shows more analysis and academic inclination. Business Administration is somewhere in between, depending upon the selectivity of your undergraduate program.

6. **Philosophy**: Again, highlight your writing and analysis skills. Great stuff, especially when you have the grades to match.

The question is this: knowing how law schools view your major, what can you do to make up for any weaknesses? If you haven't had much writing in your curriculum, try writing for your school paper or getting research published. This is just one example of using your weaknesses to build your law school applications.

They key is to pick a major that interests you and do well in it. If that major develops thinking skills, cultural interests, and passions, that is even better. The important thing is to do well at the things you undertake.

ADVICE FOR THE SCHOOL YEAR

1. **Get to know your professors**. Take the initiative to meet professors during office hours, to take more than one class with a few professors, and to assist with a professor's research interests. Obtain letters of recommendation at a time when the professor's memory of you is fresh. If letters are sent to LSDAS, (more on LSDAS in a subsequent chapter) they will be useable for five years. Be proactive about forming relationships with faculty members who will attest to your writing abilities, analytical skills, research interests, and intellectual curiosity.

2. **Don't join anything just to join**. If something really interests you, become an active leader in that organization. It doesn't have to be the pre-law club, but if it is Phi Alpha Delta, be a leader in it and not just someone who writes the name of the club on his resume after paying dues. Whether it's a cultural organization, student government, or athletics, demonstrate leadership, growth, and dedication in

your involvements, rather than simply collecting memberships in a number of different groups.

3. **Find your niche**. Use college to explore things that really interest you and find the connection between them. Do things that interest you no matter how prestigious they seem to others. Test your boundaries and stretch your horizons. Running races, teaching dance to children, photographing India's villages, and building houses for Habitat for Humanity are all worthwhile pursuits if you dedicate yourself to them.

4. **Grades always matter**. If you don't end up going to law school next year, everyone will see your senior year grades so keep going strong. Plus, if you're waitlisted somewhere and want to add something impressive to your file, there's nothing like an improved GPA in your senior year.

5. **Watch yourself on Myspace, Facebook, and google**. Be professional and exercise good judgment in presenting yourself to the public, because you are trying to show readiness to be a lawyer soon. Watch the comments on blogs that can be traced back to you, pick appropriate email addresses, and use privacy settings on your social networking pages. Someone on a waitlist at a Conservative, Christian law school recently posted a comment on my blog asking whether it might be problematic that she modeled in her bikini for a calendar. Use common sense.

6. **Stay out of trouble.** Be careful about minor-in-possession tickets, DUIs, and academic probation. Show that you can exercise good judgment by not finding yourself in these situations. If you do get

caught doing something you shouldn't have, make up for it by distancing yourself, volunteering for an awareness campaign against substance abuse, and being very careful about not getting into any more trouble.

7. **Plan to take the LSAT.** The best times are either in June after your junior year or in the fall of your senior year, and start preparing approximately three months before the exam. Plan your class, activity, and work schedule accordingly. You will need to dedicate yourself to this effort.

8. **Find meaning in what you are doing.** Don't pick a major because it "looks good" or because your father thought Accounting would be a good major for finding a job after college. You'll do better with a subject that interests and inspires you.

> Law schools embrace depth more than breadth. Explore leadership opportunities in one or two related areas, rather than simply joining five different organizations because you think it'll look good on your law school applications.

HOW TO SPEND YOUR SUMMERS

Many pre-law students ask me how they should spend their summers during college. They specifically ask whether or not they should try to work at a law firm. My advice is always that you should not take an internship at a law firm for your resume's sake. If it's really a sports agency, a non-profit, an after school program, or learning a language that interests you, spend your time in a way that shows who you really are that will encourage your growth. Law schools do not want cookie cutter students; they want students who will make meaningful contributions.

During the initial phone consultation with prospective law school admission consulting clients, often a parent or applicant will say that they've had "great internships." These invariably include things like "Semester in DC" programs, interning with a Member of Congress (which really just means answering calls and giving tours of the Capitol building, right?), or perhaps something in the business world like being a marketing and promotions intern for a sports company (which is really just throwing t-shirts into a crowd).

Where do internships come into play when building the strengths of a law school application?

Internships are better than working at The GAP. Unless, of course, you had to work at The GAP to pay your rent and tuition. Then, working at The GAP, if explained the right way in your application, shows a lot more about you than an internship with a politician would.

It's even better, however, to have had 2 or 3 internships in quasi-related fields. If you've had 2-3 internships in totally unrelated fields (public relations and finance, for example), it can look like you lack direction and haven't found your stride yet. How do you counteract some of these assumptions? Emphasize that you take initiative in the things that you do and that you learn from each opportunity. Demonstrate that you are not just a person skating through another boring summer; show that you really put the effort in to understand the field.

Don't assume your experiences are more amazing than anyone else's just because your internship sounds fancy. You should only choose to emphasize your internship in a personal statement if you learned something specific in a unique situation, were able to contribute meaningfully, or learned something significant from having a negative experience at an internship. Think about what makes the experience interesting because simply having the internship on your resume probably isn't impressive enough to a law school admission officer or law faculty member. The way to make an internship meaningful is to seek meaning in it while you are in it.

Any experience that shows initiative is good. Being self motivated, giving yourself the freedom to make mistakes and learn from them, and exercising good judgment and independent thought and action go a long way in impressing a law school. Remember this during each of your employment and internship experiences.

Consider what you can do to round out your experiences. This requires being honest with yourself and putting your mother's boasts about your accomplishments on the side burner. When you observe your experiences candidly, are you someone who has never really had to earn his own pocket money? You might benefit from gaining some work experience. Might you appear to be a little self-centered by only being active in your fraternity? Despite efforts to emphasize the group's mighty philanthropic endeavors, consider spending some time giving back to your community. Do you need to compensate for lackluster grades by demonstrating intellectual ability and maturity? How about a research project, undertaking a thesis, or becoming a tutor? Taking time for some critical introspection now will not only benefit your law school applications, but will enable your personal growth, which will only, in turn, benefit your law school applications.

Never do anything as resume filler or because you think an LOR from an attorney is your ticket into law school. Spending a summer as a file clerk or runner at a law firm gets you nothing. You are not going to get a meaningful learning experience from this position, and any resulting LOR would simply say, "He was always on time and wore a tie." If you think this kind of position will add meat to an assertion in your personal statement about why you want to go to law school, think again. After all, no one is going to believe you really gained an understanding of what lawyers do by bringing them their mail and organizing files. Well, I take that back. You might actually gain a great idea of how unglamorous the legal profession really is, but it would be hard to turn that into a captivating story for your personal statement. Not worth it. It is better to do something that shows your true interests and passions. Dedicate your precious time to something you've always wanted to explore.

CHAPTER 2

THE MAIN INGREDIENTS: LSAT & GPA

THE two most important factors in law school admission are undergraduate grade point average (UGPA) and LSAT score. There are no exceptions to this. I would be lying if I told you otherwise. These factors are the biggest predictors of your ability to succeed in law school, and that's why law schools place great emphasis on them. While there are exceptions to every statistic, law schools feed the data regarding their students to LSAC. LSAC in turn produces correlation studies to show who is making it through law school and passing the bar on the first try.

UNDERGRADUATE GRADES

Your UGPA is the cumulative GPA as computed from all of your undergraduate transcripts by the Law School Admission Council (LSAC). A law school takes these numbers and applies its specially calculated "index" formula to them. The index is based on previous students at that school and how they fared academically and on the bar exam. It is supposed to predict the likelihood of you performing well in law school and passing the state's bar on the first try.

Your undergraduate grades are, if I'm being honest, the

second most important piece of the puzzle. Even if a school claims to count LSAT and GPA equally, the GPA is subject to a lot more subjectivity than the LSAT score. The factors that add miniature pluses and minuses to your GPA in the minds of the admission officers include:

- **Caliber of School**: A 3.3 at UCLA is different than a 3.3 at Random State University Lacking National Reputation.
- **Difficulty Level of Course Load**: A 3.3 in Chemical Engineering is different than a 3.3 in Political Science.
- **Grades**: Was your 3.3 the result of As and Cs or Bs across the board? (Some excellence is preferred over consistent mediocrity).
- **Repeating Courses**: Does your school GPA of 3.3 include repeated courses? If so, beware! LSAC might calculate your GPA differently than many under-graduate schools do. Also, credits you took at other institutions (even college credits earned while in high school) might impact your GPA.
- **Upward Trend**: Is your 3.3 the result of a slow start, ending with 3.7 and 3.8 in your last two years? Did your grades consistently improve each semester? Schools are more likely to forgive a rough start than a rough finish. Maturity and growth are always a good sell to law schools. (Exceptions to this might include increased family or professional responsibilities).
- **Study Abroad**: Does your school GPA include studying abroad credits? In most cases, LSAC uses them to compute your GPA. Subjectively, schools will consider whether you studied for a summer in

England versus a year in a third-world country taking classes in a foreign language.

- **Work Experience**: Was your 3.3 GPA earned while working 25 hours per week? Schools take into account the hours you worked during school. Working for 5-10 hours a week at a bar or coffee shop at various points during college won't excuse lackluster grades, but working to put yourself through school definitely adds a dimension to comprehending your transcripts more meaningfully.

- **Distinguishing Yourself Academically**: Was your 3.3 supplemented by intensive research or writing? Schools like to see a student who demonstrated a sincere interest in academia by writing a thesis or presenting a paper at a conference. If you successfully petition to write an honors thesis even though your GPA didn't qualify you, this can help make up for a lackluster GPA.

It is important to note that classes you took after receiving your undergraduate degree do not count toward the GPA that LSAC computes for you. Additional courses taken after you have a bachelor degree, whether at the college or graduate level or toward a paralegal degree, do not count in the GPA. They might be considered as "soft factors" or "plus factors" but not as part of your official GPA for law school application purposes.

THE LSAT

The LSAT is administered by the Law School Admission Council (LSAC). It is a standardized exam that requires significant preparation. It is not something you can take blind or cold.

It is an aptitude exam. What this means is that some people will naturally do better on this exam than others. I often tell my clients that I'm a reasonably bright person, graduated near the top of my law school class, was graduation speaker, a member of Order of the Coif and law review, but even if I studied for a year for the test I probably would not get a 95th percentile score. I'm ok with that, and so should you be if that's the case for you. However, unless you prepare adequately, you will not receive the score that truly measures your aptitude.

Because it's not a knowledge-based test, the way to be successful is to prepare enough so that you obtain your best score. If you study for 2-3 months and hit a stride where you're consistently scoring in a 5-8 point range, that is probably the score that is right for you and you should craft a strategy for selecting a law school based on that score. However, "If your score is all over the place, you haven't fully integrated a strategy and you'll be going into the test leaving your score to chance," according to Bara Sapir, founder and executive director of Test Prep New York.

WHY IS THE LSAT SO DARN IMPORTANT?

The LSAT is the only objective piece of your law school application. It is the only way you will be judged exactly equally with everyone else. There are three exceptions to this:

1. **If you received accommodations for the LSAT.**
    LSAC is notoriously stingy with accommodations. Whereas colleges may be scared of lawsuits from disabled students, LSAC apparently is not. An accommodated LSAT score is as of this printing not one that schools must report to the ABA. Therefore,

accommodated test scores do not impact a school's ranking in U.S. News & World Report. However, an accommodated score does not mean a school has great incentive to admit you unless everything else in your application is stellar. Also, you will have to choose whether to disclose the nature of and reason for your accommodation to the law school. There can be drawbacks. If your disability will make practicing law rather difficult, you will need to assure the schools that it will not be a problem in practice. After all, judges don't give extra time for submitting motions because you have a disability, and clients don't allow you to double bill because it takes you longer to read cases. You'll want to assure law schools you've created survival skills for yourself and that you won't be a high maintenance law student.

2. **If something strange happened during the LSAT**. Did you have the flu? Was a family member admitted to the hospital that week? Did the person next to you at the LSAT have a seizure? While a school won't ignore your LSAT score under these circumstances, it can be convincing to explain why you would have done better (and hopefully did do better eventually upon retaking the examination) under different circumstances.

3. **If you have a history of underperformance on standardized tests.** This does not mean that you simply wish you had done better than you did. This means that you have a history of very low standardized test scores (especially as compared to your classmates in college) but that you excelled academically (performed

much better than most of your classmates in college). If you do have this kind of spotty history, Ms. Sapir says that it is paramount to take stock as to *why*. She says, "It is not uncommon that test anxiety is the culprit, and eliminating it from your test taking practice is very easy. You might start by talking with your doctor or taking up new methods that are relaxation inducing."

TIPS FOR GETTING YOUR BEST LSAT SCORE

<u>Plan to take the test once and only once</u>. Although LSAC allows you to take the test three times in a two year period (it is offered four times a year – in February, June, September/October, and December), and allows for a fourth test administration if you obtain special permission from a law school, you really want to take it only once. Here are the reasons why:

- It's time consuming to prepare.
- It's expensive to prepare and to take.
- Many law schools average multiple scores.
- Delaying the LSAT means delaying the review of your applications by law schools, which means losing priority in the rolling admission process.

WAYS TO PREPARE FOR THE LSAT

It has become standard for people to take preparatory courses or seek a tutor to assist with LSAT preparation. The big test preparation companies are Princeton Review, Kaplan, Test Masters, Testmasters180, Powerscore, and Blueprint. These companies tend to take a one-size-fits-all approach to test prep, but with systems that are effective for many people and courses that are widely available geographically and online.

> For more about preparing for the LSAT, see "101 Ways to a Higher LSAT Score" by Linda C. Ashar featuring a 3 page case study I provided.

A full-length prep course is a big investment of time and money. If you know you won't be able to attend the classes and do the homework, this is probably not the option for you. If you're not self-motivated, these programs may not be effective for you. I find that my clients who struggle with standardized testing really suffer in the big courses like Kaplan and Princeton Review and are frustrated with their lack of progress during the course.

There are many smaller locally-based programs available. Definitely do your research. Depending on your work, school, and family commitments, you may find that tutoring works better for you. Companies such as Integrated Learning and Test Prep New York are based upon personalized programs and one-on-one tutoring. There are also tutors in every major city advertising their services on http://www.craigslist.org.

> My #1 study tip for practice LSAT questions: Review every answer, even if you got that question right. After all, you might've gotten it right by accident!

Some things to be aware of before signing up for any test prep course or tutor:

- Talk to people who have completed the program and ask them about the program's strengths and weaknesses. If possible, talk to people who had the same instructor or tutor that you will have, because the person teaching the course makes a big difference in how the material is presented and whether it will make sense for your learning style.

- Find out what happens if the instructor gets sick or quits mid-session.

- Look into how stringent the requirements are to qualify for the course "guarantee." Ask how many homework assignments, quizzes, and in-class sessions will you need to complete to be eligible for this benefit. "If the course didn't work the first time, it will most likely not work a second time," says Ms. Sapir. Chances of light bulbs going off and suddenly "getting it" the second time around are not great.

- In addition to the instructor's LSAT score, find out the instructor's teaching experience. Just like brilliant faculty members are occasionally terrible teachers, brilliant LSAT takers cannot necessarily transfer that skill to others.

- Do your homework and shop around for pricing, availability, and convenience. Make sure you feel a rapport with the person who will be tutoring you. You shouldn't feel intimidated.

- Be aware of "sales-y" language or unreasonable promises. This is probably the one and only time I'll advise you to check law school discussion forums. I recently saw a message thread with students wondering about a specific tutor, followed by a really cocky and unprofessional response from that tutor. You're entering a profession; pick a professional.

There are also self-study options. Many of my clients swear by the Powerscore Bibles. If you study on your own, it's essential to practice with actual LSAT tests under timed conditions, including allowance for the experimental section of the test. This is all about endurance. Steve Schwartz, a professional LSAT tutor in New York City, offers the following advice for self-study, "Create a reasonable but demanding study schedule and stick to it. Hold yourself accountable for time you miss. If your exam date is 2-3 months away, don't let more than a couple of days go by without using your LSAT books. Preparing for the LSAT is, at a minimum, a part-time job. It will require dedication and consistent attention, but the payoff can be tremendous."

How Do You Know if You're Really Ready for the LSAT?

If you don't feel ready to take the LSAT, your instinct is probably right. You have a few options. You could take the test and if your score is halfway decent, you can apply. This is a poor strategy that usually goes worse than you expected and becomes something you have to later explain on your applications. Plus, it's a huge ego-deflater to see a low score. Make sure to take many timed practice tests with five sections. It's an endurance test and a speed test, so you must practice under these conditions. Practice in distracting conditions, not in ideal ones. It is better to take a test in a noisy coffee shop than in the silence and ideal environment of a library carrel of the 7th floor of your campus library.

Preparing for Test Day

One of my clients talked to friends about where they had taken the test and chose her test site based on their feedback about the location. Early registration is important for popular sites. Check out the location ahead of time. Try to see what kind of desks are in the room and where in the room you might be most comfortable. When choosing your seat on test day, stay away from doors and high traffic areas, including the proctor's desk, which is usually noisy and distracting. Likewise, be flexible enough not to panic if seating is assigned.

Be ready to roll with the punches on LSAT day. It may take an hour for the proctor to read the instructions and that might leave you pretty hungry come break time. The person next to you might clear his throat ten times per section. I almost guarantee the proctor will be talkative, overly social, and clueless. Expect the worst and do not let anything throw you.

Multiple LSAT Scores

No matter how well prepared you might feel for the LSAT, crazy things happen on test day. You may decide to cancel your score, or wait for your score and then decide whether to retake the exam. Therefore, it's important to consider your options.

As of June 2006, law schools have an incentive to weigh only the highest of multiple LSAT scores because of a new ABA policy. Therefore, the only downsides to retaking it are: (1) time spent studying; (2) cost; (3) delay in getting your applications reviewed; and (4) the possibility that you might have to explain to a law school why your score decreased the second time.

I refer to schools ranked as "Third" or "Fourth" tier in U.S. News and World Reports rankings as Regional law schools because this the purpose of these schools is to enable the local population to obtain a legal education and to go on to take the Bar exam and practice law in the community, state, or region where the law school is located. This doesn't mean you are stuck in this region after graduation, but it does explain why a lot of these schools are punished by U.S. News' rankings, because they do not generally recruit applicants in the same way that national law schools do, so these schools are at a disadvantage in the criteria utilized by rankings.

Almost all law school applicants are disappointed with their score on their first LSAT. Many times, people feel like they will be walking around with their bad score pinned to their foreheads for the entirety of their legal careers. The question is, how disappointed are you? I listen to my clients and determine from speaking to them whether the circumstances surrounding their score make it likely they would improve on a second attempt. There is no hard and fast rule that applies to everyone.

It's important to consider that some schools claim to "average" multiple LSAT scores and some claim to take the highest of multiple scores. What this means is that a school follows its particular philosophy when choosing what numbers go into its index calculation. However, schools also employ subjective determinations in making admission decisions, and an improved score and a good explanation for a lower score shouldn't count against you and will help overcome the school's presumption of averaging multiple scores.

A few years ago, every school averaged multiple scores and hardly anyone retook the LSAT as a result. When the ABA changed the way scores would be reported, and therefore the way scores would be counted in the all-important U.S. News and World Report rankings, it changed how most schools count the scores. This is a good thing for applicants who are able to improve their scores, but it also results in many more people retaking the LSAT, making it even more important to start earlier in the admission cycle in case you decide later to follow this route.

Canceling an LSAT Score

Will this hurt you? No. It just puts that much pressure on you for next time. So, when should you cancel? If you completely screw up by leaving an entire section blank, misbubble the last ten questions, or become violently ill in the middle of the exam, you should probably cancel. This is especially true if the score would be so demoralizing to you that you would be unable to live with yourself. Another reason to cancel is if you already have one LSAT score that you're content with and you're pretty sure you don't want to have to explain to law schools why the second score is lower.

You should not cancel a score if you want to apply for early decision, early notification, or otherwise take advantage of the rolling admissions process and get things underway early. Also, if you leave feeling unsure about your performance but know you didn't absolutely panic or make any major mistakes, you should keep your score. Another situation in which you should not cancel would be if you felt you made a slight error or were unable to finish a question or two, but nothing out of the ordinary happened to throw your concentration or ability to perform.

THE TRUTH ABOUT VERY LOW LSAT SCORES

This is, unfortunately, the most popular topic on my blog. Therefore, I would be remiss if I did not address this issue here. I am informally known as the beacon of hope for people who score under a 150 on the LSAT or even those in the low or mid-150s who hope to go to top 30 schools. This fame is because I have testimonials on my web site from people with 140s LSAT scores who sing my praises and give me all of the credit for their acceptance to law school. It should be understood that these are very select clients. When someone with a low LSAT history calls me, I screen them carefully to determine whether they have other factors going for them, and only if they do will I take them on as a client.

If your LSAT is under 150, you are absolutely looking at regional law schools. If your LSAT is under 150 and you're insisting on going to a top law school, you will not be successful. That's all there is to it. I won't sugarcoat that for anyone. You then have three choices: (1) re-take the LSAT and improve your score, (2) be more flexible in your schools list, or (3) re-think your plans to attend law school.

Some blunt and honest truths about low-LSAT applicants (with few exceptions):

- If you have a high 140s LSAT, a solid GPA (3.5+ overall), and no other big problems in your background, if you apply to the right schools for you and submit the best possible application materials, you will probably be successful.
- If your grades are terrible (2.5 and under) and your LSAT is under 150, you will face an uphill battle

getting into any law school. Possible exceptions include 10-20 years of professional experience, a reputable graduate degree with a high GPA and a strong faculty letter of recommendation, dire financial circumstances or health circumstances during college that have since been resolved, or (and I hate to say this, but it's true) you are a member of a group considered to be an underrepresented minority.

- If you have a 130s LSAT, you're not going to be successful. Exceptions? Very, very rare. In fact, while I was director of admissions at a regional law school I accepted only two applicants with LSATs under 140 and, mind you, this was almost 10 years ago. One acceptance was a young man who was completely self-made, grew up as an orphaned immigrant, got himself out of juvenile hall and to college, and scored a high GPA in a tough major at a good school. The second person, I'm embarrassed to admit, was an accident. I checked the wrong box on her application. Both made it through law school and passed the bar, but the odds were against them.

If you fall into the "Very Low LSAT" category, what should you do?

1. Think long and hard about why you got that score and whether or not it's something you can correct by increasing your preparation time or changing your preparation methods.
2. Think about what the law degree is worth to you and do your research to be sure this is really the profession

for you before you commit yourself to further expense and investment of time.

3. Don't hire anyone to help you who absolutely guarantees your success in the law school admission process. I know how much hope you hold out for anyone who says there is even a possibility, but be very guarded with your dollars and your optimism.

4. Please, please, please do not apply late in the cycle. Then you are really shooting yourself in the foot.

5. Choose schools wisely. If a school never takes anyone with your LSAT score, no matter how amazing your personal statement, life story, or letters of recommendation, you are not going to be admitted to that school. If a school regularly takes people with your numbers, even if it doesn't accept very many people, give it a shot early in the admission cycle with the best possible application you can create.

6. Don't expect the same behavior to bring about different results. If you do plan to retake the LSAT, only do so if you're willing to invest the time and money necessary to really improve the outcome.

Where can you find out a law school's admission criteria? The ABA LSAC Official Guide to ABA-Approved Law Schools is published each year by the Law School Admission Council and the American Bar Association. It states the 25th and 75th percentile numbers for each ABA school and many schools are kind enough to provide a chart of how many people they admitted in each GPA/LSAT bracket.

Part-time Programs as an Option For Applicants with Lower LSAT Scores

Many law school applicants try to use part-time programs as a "back door" to law school admission. It's true that for those schools that offer part-time programs, the entering GPA and LSAT numbers are often lower than for the full time program at the same school. However, the difference is usually only slight, just a point or two on the LSAT. If your LSAT is ten points under the 25th percentile for the part-time program, simply applying part-time isn't going to be what makes the difference in your admission decision. Applying part-time may increase your chances of being admitted, but only if your numbers are more in line with those of the part-time admitted students.

Conditional Programs

One option for students with low LSAT scores is to try to obtain admission to a school's conditional program. At schools that offer this program, it's usually a four-week trial run, either at the campus or online. You take a law school course or two, and if you meet a certain grade threshold you are invited to join the fall class as an admitted student. These programs are a great way into law school for those students whose struggle with the LSAT is not an adequate predictor of academic success in law school. However, these programs are expensive and time consuming, and more students leave without an acceptance letter than leave with one.

You want to know going into the program how many people participated in the previous year's program and how many were admitted. If a lot were admitted, I'd then want to know how many were academically dismissed from law school during or following their first year of the program. Go into this with open eyes, because if you don't make it through the program successfully, it will be even harder to obtain admission to another school when you try applying to law school in the future.

Chapter 3

WORKING THE ROLLING
ADMISSIONS PROCESS

"ROLLING Admissions" is a phrase that causes confusion in some, and fails to register at all with others. A potential client considering applying to law schools in February/March asked me which schools operate on "rolling admissions." She seemed shocked when I answered, "All of them but Yale." She obviously didn't understand the term, "rolling admissions." I asked her what she meant by this phrase and she thought it meant that a school accepted applicants for a January or May start, rather than just beginning law school in the fall semester.

On the opposite end of the spectrum, someone asked me: "Is it true that you have a better shot at a long-shot school if you apply at the end of the admission cycle? I've heard that you have a better shot of getting into the 'maybe' pile this way." My response was (literally and unapologetically), "That's the most ridiculous thing I've ever heard." Why would a law school want a procrastinator who shows poor judgment about his chances of getting into their school? Why would they take a late applicant over someone they've already waitlisted who applied nice and early, thereby showing serious interest in the school? Why would a law school make room for someone at the end of the application cycle unless he or she brings something to the class that wouldn't otherwise be represented there?

What is evident from these questions is that it's very important to understand what rolling admissions is all about. Your future is ahead of you, and September-November is the time to grab it. Most law schools start accepting applications on September 1, and almost every law school operates on a rolling admissions system. What does this mean? Law schools give away seats throughout the year. There are more seats available at the beginning of the cycle when law schools aren't sure they'll be able to fill their class, and there are fewer seats available once the law school has already reviewed thousands of applications. Makes sense, right?

Even if a school says it accepts applications through June, it doesn't mean it's a good idea to apply in the spring. Although some schools keep their options open to let in that person with the 175 LSAT, 3.9 GPA, and stellar record, the June deadline is not for the mid-range applicants.

That being said, do you need to apply on the first possible day? No. Should you? No. Here's why: first, law school admission officers are off recruiting people to apply to their law school. They aren't spending their time in September reviewing very many files. Take time to attend a local law forum (sponsored by LSAC in major cities) or law fair at a local university. Shake some hands, collect some information, ask questions, just not dumb questions. Time and time again when it was my job to stand behind the recruiting table I was asked, "What is your medium LSAT score?" The second reason is that the office is still getting up to speed on its processes, data clerks are learning, changes are being implemented, and LSDAS is trying new things. Let them work out the kinks a bit instead of experimenting on your file.

WHEN TO SUBMIT APPLICATIONS

Rather than applying on the first day a school accepts applications, take a few extra weeks and make sure you're submitting a quality product instead of a rushed one, and get the application submitted in <u>October</u>. I consider any application submitted by mid-October to be early, and any application submitted before Thanksgiving to be sufficiently early to take advantage of rolling admissions.

"I have been at three law schools in which the school experienced a 30-plus percent increase in application volume," Charles Roboski, Assistant Dean of Admission and Financial Aid at Michigan State University College of Law, told me. "At each school, we ended up "tightening" admission standards after realizing that the increase would be sustained....usually in January. Hence, some candidates with a solid profile who applied in October/November were admitted in December, but other candidates with identical credentials were waitlisted or denied when applying in February."

This is not to say that any application submitted in December is a waste, but it's a little bit less advantageous and will mean a longer wait before you hear back from schools. Any application submitted after the first of January is begging to be a waitlist candidate at best unless it's a safety school. January is no time to apply if you have complicated issues such as a criminal record or honor code violation in your file that mean your application will take longer to review.

WHEN TO TAKE THE LSAT

Your LSAT date is the key piece of the puzzle in committing to a timetable for submitting your applications. There are two important things to remember about LSAT timing: (1) your file will not be reviewed without an LSAT score, and (2) it takes approximately three weeks for LSAT scores to be emailed out after the test date. This impacts your ability to come up with a reasonable schools list, and also to study for the next LSAT administration should you decide to re-take the test.

With these two factors in mind, you need to decide when to take the LSAT. It's offered 4 times a year: February, June, September or October, and December.

> The fall LSAT administration sometimes falls at the end of September and sometimes at the beginning of October. I refer to the September LSAT and October LSAT interchangeably throughout this book.

THE BEST LSAT ADMINISTRATION
IS IN JUNE

If you are a junior in college planning to attend law school immediately after you graduate (as opposed to taking a year or more off from school), you should take the June LSAT before your senior year. There are two reasons for this and two exceptions.

Advantages to taking the June LSAT:

1. Having your score in time to spend the summer deciding upon a schools list and getting your materials

ready so applications can be submitted early in the rolling admissions process (September of your senior year); and

2. Having the luxury of retaking the LSAT (if necessary and/or advisable) in October of your senior year so that you can still apply early and take advantage of rolling admissions.

Two Exceptions to the June LSAT Rule:

1. If your school/work/activities schedule prohibits you from studying for the test in the March-June timeframe.

2. If your school is on the quarter system and you'll be in finals during the June LSAT administration.

If you are a senior and just getting started in the admission process, September is the best time to take the LSAT. Study over the summer before your senior year. If you're deciding on law school and you're already in your senior year, you're left with the December LSAT. Make this a priority during your fall semester, and put extracurricular activities on the back burner because most college seniors are taking difficult courses. I consider the December LSAT the "LSAT of Last Resort." You won't get your score until the holidays and you'll be spending your winter break on applications. There's nothing inherently wrong with this plan other than it being a less desirable time of the year to apply (again, rolling admissions). But, if you get the flu over winter break or your family has the audacity to want to spend time with you or take you on some fabulous vacation, this plan will have its hiccups and delays.

WHY THE FEBRUARY LSAT
IS NOT A GOOD IDEA

The only "good" way to take the February LSAT is as someone who is: (1) already done with school; (2) has lots of time in November-January to prepare; and (3) is not applying for the current admission cycle but for the next one after that. For example, taking the February 2010 LSAT for Fall 2011 admission would be the smart way. Of course, most nontraditional applicants are in a hurry to start law school once they make up their minds to do so and the idea of waiting out 18 months feels like 18 years. However, if you're a recent college graduate who plans to take exactly two years off after graduation, you are probably the perfect candidate for the February LSAT, which falls about 7-8 months after graduation in most cases. Taking this test buys you the spring and summer to continue to build your experience and the pieces of your applications, putting you on the ideal timeline for law school admissions. It also means the schools will see your last year of grades, hopefully showing continued dedication to your studies.

The "bad" way to take the February LSAT is for admission the following fall. I know many schools say they accept the February LSAT, but this really only works well for people who know they are applying only to a few key schools in their geographic area and who have a pretty good idea that their scores will make them competitive at those schools. Trying to come up with a schools list without an LSAT score is a nightmare. You'll end up applying to schools with little rhyme, reason, or indication of the possibility of success. It is very important to submit applications before your February LSAT score is received. Again, the pesky rolling admission process comes into play here, and the actual deadlines tend to be Feb. 1, Feb. 15, or March 1 for many schools.

Taking the February LSAT for fall admission reeks of desperation. It's a last ditch effort. Of course, there are often legitimate reasons that people find themselves in such a desperate situation. You might've planned for December but didn't feel prepared, you might've gotten the flu, misbubbled the score sheet, or been seated next to someone with an annoying cough, so there's a reason LSAC offers the test in February. But, a February LSAT score never puts you in a position of strength. It may get you into law school, but it would be a last-ditch, "let's see what happens, I can always try again next year" kind of application. People do get into law schools with February LSAT scores, but not as often as they would with an earlier "complete" date on the application.

Taking the June LSAT
for Admission that Fall

Planning to take your first LSAT in June for admission the following fall is a losing proposition unless you're the one-in-a-million person who will get a score that puts you above a school's 75th percentile and you have the GPA and credentials to match. Even schools that say they'll accept the June LSAT don't necessarily give equal consideration to people who applied eight months before. Plus, schools are already hitting their waitlists at that point, so what would be their incentive to take a new applicant?

Is there a reason to re-take the LSAT in June? Yes, if you're desperate to bring up one or two previous low scores and you're pretty darn sure you can improve and get yourself in the running numbers-wise. But if you're still not going to hit a school's numbers, retaking the LSAT in June isn't going to get you anywhere. One possible exception to this might be a part-time program.

The other reason to take the LSAT in June is if you're on a waitlist and you feel confident in your ability to raise your score enough to make the difference. I had a client with a 165 who was waitlisted at Northwestern. He took the LSAT again while on the waitlist in June and came back with a 170 and an acceptance letter.

PART II

APPLYING TO LAW SCHOOL

CREATING YOUR APPLICATION TIMELINE

NOW that you know when you want to apply, work backward to create a timeline for yourself. Trust me, effective law school applications cannot be thrown together in a week, and some of the things over which you maintain the least amount of control, such as letters of recommendation and transcripts, take the longest to obtain. Both LORs and transcripts must be sent to LSDAS, the service of LSAC that forwards this information to each law school you apply to. Therefore, YES, you must register for LSDAS immediately, and YES, you must pay the $12 fee for each law school you apply to so that your LSDAS report (which includes LSAT score(s), transcripts, an LSAC calculated Academic Summary Report, and letters of recommendation) can be forwarded to each school.

> *Budget smartly for application fees. "I did not realize how expensive applications are," said one of my clients. "I paid over $1,000 to LSAC alone for my entire process including taking the LSAT, registering with LSDAS, test preparation, applications, and LSAC reports."*

Your personal application timeline is built around your LSAT date. Get started on transcripts, LORs, resume, and essays right away. If you already have an LSAT score and you are just waiting for a second score, you might consider submitting some applications before you get your score. Just save room in the application budget for additional applications once you know your new score. No one will review your application without an LSAT score, but at least it can be processed. Be careful though. If you're waiting for a second score, be sure to tell the schools. Mistakes happen all the time where schools reject someone who is waiting for a second LSAT score. Don't trust that schools will pay attention to an upcoming LSAT date on your application if you already have one score on record. Tell the schools to wait for your second score and then, once LSAC shows that the second score has been sent, call the school and make sure it was added to your file. Every year, I have clients rejected and waitlisted and schools that promised to hold their decision. One of these schools was actually a Top 5. Don't assume law schools are always right. If this happens to you, there is no reason to panic. Schools will usually agree to put your file through another review.

CHAPTER 4

LETTERS OF RECOMMENDATION

THE first thing to do is to get LORs underway. It takes time to consider the right person, ask that person, supply him or her with the appropriate information and materials, and then wait for that person to write your letter and send it to LSDAS. Then, of course, you have to wait for LSDAS to process it.

You can't decide who should write an LOR on your behalf without understanding its role in the admission process. The LOR provides law schools with a third party's assessment of your strengths and background. The right LOR adds credibility to your application. A mediocre one is a lost opportunity to have a trusted individual echo the themes of your application.

THE BEST LOR IS THE ACADEMIC LOR

The most important thing law schools want to know from an LOR is that you can handle the academic rigor of law school. Your undergraduate and graduate school professors are the best people to speak to this.

A strong professor LOR includes an explanation of how the professor knows you and in what context. What classes did you take with her? When? She should describe how well she got to know you. Were you one of 200 but you stood out because you visited her during office hours weekly? Were you graded on essays? Multiple choice tests? Did you write papers? About what? How well were they written and researched? How did you present yourself and your ideas in front of the class? How did you do when your ideas were challenged? The letter should give an indication that you took academics seriously, did real work rather than simply skating through a course with little effort, and should demonstrate that the professor respects you. If the professor can come out and say, "I've taught hundreds of students who have gone on to top 20 law schools, and Jane stands out in the top 2% of those students in terms of writing and analytical ability, and is in the top 5 in terms of oratory skills…," it's a great letter. Of course, what makes this a great letter is that it's hard to get, even if you're a strong student. Classes are large, professors are overworked, and it's difficult to shine under these circumstances.

> *In most circumstances, give a professor 4-6 weeks and a boss 2-4 weeks to write your letter of recommendation.*

It's especially important to have an academic letter in the following situations:

1. Showing that the As did not come easily to you; you worked for them.
2. If you have a lackluster overall GPA, a strong professor letter helps overcome doubts about your academic abilities.

HOW TO ASK A PROFESSOR FOR A LOR

If you still have time before applying to law school, try to take multiple classes from one or two of the same professors. This gives the professor an opportunity to know you better and comment about your performance more meaningfully. Ideally, law school applicants should develop relationships with faculty while taking classes rather than trying to fabricate them at the last minute when LORs are due. Cultivate the relationship. Maybe stop by office hours 2-3 times before asking for the LOR. Perhaps even ask the professor to join you for a cup of coffee so you have the opportunity to discuss your goals, concerns, hopes, and direction.

When you ask a professor to write you a LOR, do it in person during office hours, and not right as the professor is setting up to teach class in a few minutes. Faculty members might ask to see your personal statement and resume before writing you a letter of recommendation. As a director of admissions, I never liked to see a LOR that mentioned anything that person would not have known first hand. Anything echoing or repeating the personal statement or resume is a complete waste of the LOR, which is intended to provide an objective third-party perspective to the application. If the professor knows about your work with a student organization as the faculty advisor for that organization, that is within the bounds of an LOR, but if it's something the professor only knows from you, it's not worth including.

LSDAS makes you designate a LOR as either "General" or "Targeted" and I see a lot of applicants confused about these terms. The only time to use a Targeted LOR is if the writer is mentioning a specific law school in the letter. What are reasons to do this? If the writer is a graduate of that school or taught there or has some other very significant tie to the institution, then a targeted letter is appropriate. As of early 2009, LSDAS allows you, and in fact requires you, to select which letters to send to each school.

A better solution? Give the professor bullet point reminders of the work you did in the class(es) he or she taught, including papers, tests, presentations, and any conversations you had during office hours or before or after class. If you worked twenty hours a week during school, it can be helpful to tell the professor so he or she can say something along the lines of, "In fact, her dedication to academic excellence was so consistent that I was surprised to learn only recently about her tremendous work schedule and household responsibilities." Talking to the professor about your career goals, even if they are vague and more along the lines of seeking a continuing intellectual challenge, is also helpful. Professors become disenchanted with students whom they perceive to expect praise without delivering quality work and who simply coast through school. It goes a long way to show a professor that you're not one of those students.

What do you do if your Professor seems lukewarm about the prospect of writing a letter on your behalf? She hems and haws and sort of turns the responsibility back to you. "*You'll need to give me your resume and the final draft of your personal statement, and I'm going to Timbuktu tomorrow so it'll be about four months before I can get to it."*

Your impulse should be to run away quickly. Your response, however, should be as follows:

"Thank you so much for making the time to do this for me when you have so much going on. Unfortunately, I really was hoping to have my applications complete in the next four weeks. Perhaps if I'm waitlisted somewhere I could ask you again in the spring?"

A lukewarm letter "Iz No Gud," as they said in *My Big Fat Greek Wedding.* I'd rather see an applicant with just two great letters than two great ones and a third that says, *"Jessica was prompt, attended class regularly, and seems like a nice, bright student."*

> My father, Stephen T. Kowel, Ph.D., a college Dean and professor for more than 40 years, says this is my best advice about LORs. His exact words were: "At the slightest hint of hesitation, bolt!"

NON-FACULTY OPTIONS FOR LORS

Now, before you beat yourself up over not knowing a professor able to wax poetic about you, remember that this is the strongest kind of letter because it's also the hardest to get. If you have been out of school for a while, or attended a large public university with 500 people in each class, don't get discouraged. Good options for LORs do exist.

For example, a teaching assistant may be better able to write you a detailed letter of recommendation. This is completely appropriate and the professor may even be willing to sign the letter in addition to the T.A.

If you have one or two academic LORs but are stumped for the third letter, you need to think about what else you bring to the table. Is there someone from work? Is there a supervisor, a client, or a vendor who can speak to your accomplishments and abilities? Is there a community service organization in which you've participated meaningfully?

GOOD LORs FOR NON-TRADITIONAL APPLICANTS

LORs present a common problem for non-traditional law school applicants. It's difficult to find the right person to write an LOR when you've been out of school for more than a few years and you want to keep your intention to leave your job a secret from your boss. One suggestion is to consider taking a graduate level course or two in order to obtain a more recent academic LOR and perhaps demonstrate a specific academic interest or writing ability that might not be evident from your current transcripts.

If you are agonizing over this and even thinking about not applying simply because you don't know who to ask for an LOR, it should help to know that this is the least important area of your application. The only time a LOR makes or breaks a file is when it breaks a file. If the letter is terrible, you are in trouble, because one of the reasons LORs aren't so important is because they are generally favorable. A mediocre or unflattering letter is the kiss of death in an application; it doesn't exactly boost your credibility with the admission committee.

If you have been out of school for more than two years

or are otherwise unable to obtain a letter of recommendation from a professor, the next people to look to for LORs are people who supervised you in meaningful activities. For most people, this is a supervisor who can speak in specific terms about your responsibilities, writing, communication, and presentation skills, experience problem solving, supervising others, handling difficult tasks, and willingness to work as part of, and lead, a team. If you have significant volunteer experience, someone who supervised you in that capacity may also be qualified to write a letter on your behalf.

WRITING YOUR OWN LOR

It's very likely that an employer or supervisor will ask you to write your own letter of recommendation for his or her signature. Don't let this freak you out. Instead, here's a brief outline of how to approach it:

First paragraph: Outline the writer's experience. Provide facts demonstrating the context in which the writer knows you, including his supervisory role and the length of time he has known you.

Second-Fourth paragraphs: Share factual examples of characteristics that you exhibit. For example, mention a time you demonstrated problem solving abilities, your writing skills, or your willingness to put in long hours. Make sure the writer only states things he knows about you personally and not about anything unrelated to his capacity as your supervisor. Factual details are the key to enriching a LOR, not general statements about "communication skills." Instead, include examples of times you proved those skills by drafting correspondence to clients or making a presentation in front of community leaders.

Concluding paragraph: The writer should highly recommend you for law school and offer to be available by phone to answer any questions.

LORs to Avoid at All Costs

1. The Family Friend

No family friend letters. None. Under any circumstances. (Note: **you are not** the exception to this rule). Why am I so insistent on this point? It goes back to the purpose an LOR needs to fulfill to help make your application stronger. *The writer is the only person who gets to talk in your application other than YOU.* Your letter writer must say things about you that he or she knows from personal experience. This is what adds credibility to the things you're saying about yourself in other parts of the application. The content of the LOR must be relevant to your law school application; the person you babysat for is not in a position to evaluate any of those qualities.

I don't care if the person is your dad's best friend and the mayor, or if the person was a dean at a nearby college, the answer remains the same. It's just not what law schools are looking for in evaluating your potential as a law student and a lawyer.

Even if your parents are pressuring you to ask their well-meaning, successful friends for LORs, please say, "Thanks, but no thanks." Why can't that nice judge who has played golf with your dad for 25 years write a letter? Think about what he might say, because trust me, I've read it:

"As a friend of Joey's father for the past 22 years, I have heard stories of Joey's progress during our weekly golf outings. I have seen Joey grow from a young boy to a college student who is bright and inquisitive. He is unfailingly polite and his parents are very proud of his accomplishments at (fill-in-the-blank) college. It is my understanding he did very well on his LSATs and that he has been active in community service and in his church. I am confident he will make an outstanding law student."

BLECH. You must find someone better to write a letter. Scared of burning a bridge when someone already offered to write a letter? Tell him, if you're applying to the law school he attended, it would be so nice if he might make a phone call on your behalf after your application is complete at the school. Or try saying, "Can I take you up on that in case I get wait-listed somewhere?"

3. **The Internship Supervisor**

   Stay away from LORs based on internships unless you took the lead on a project or acted in some way beyond the standard intern. If you were offered paid employment after the end of your internship, even better. The letter should be written by the person who most closely supervised your work and can add the most substantive detail to the letter, not necessarily the most famous person in the office who barely remembers meeting you. The fact that you had the impressive internship is (hopefully) well described on your resume, so only use an internship LOR if its substance will truly add value to the application by showing how you stood out, rather than simply echoing your resume and serving as confirmation that yes, you actually had the internship you said you did.

4. Graduates of the Law School

Yes, it's nice to know someone who graduated from the law school you want to attend. However, unless that person supervised you or taught you, it's not the right person to submit a LOR on your behalf. In the case where the individual continues a connection with the school or admission office, a phone call or email on your behalf is a better idea.

WAIVING YOUR RIGHT TO SEE THE LETTER

When LSDAS asks you whether you want to waive your right to see the letter, absolutely and unequivocally check the box that says "yes." The writer may still elect to share the contents of the letter with you. Checking the box tells the school you won't sue to get a copy of the letter. This adds credibility to the letter because the writer is free to be candid in his or her assessment on your credentials.

CHAPTER 5

TRANSCRIPTS TO LSDAS

Check the LSDAS website for information about which transcripts (study abroad, college credits, graduate institutions, etc.) need to be sent. Follow the directions exactly so your applications are not held up later by any inconsistencies. Trust me, there is no hiding from the summer school classes you paid for but never really attended. Remember that you can always update your transcripts as additional grades are received, so there is no need to wait for a particular term's grades to post at your school. Applicants often make the mistake of waiting for December's grades to apply to law school, but this is not necessary even if you're trying to show a continued upward trend in grades, because you are able to update your transcripts while your application is under review, at least until the point when a decision is made.

Once LSDAS processes your transcripts, take a close look at your Academic Summary Report (the document created by LSDAS that summarizes your transcripts). Check for any discrepancies. Often, the cumulative and degree GPAs are slightly different from those on your transcripts. The most common reasons for this are repeated courses (the second grade may not count for LSDAS), and study abroad or transfer credits that didn't factor into your school's calculations but do factor into LSDAS' calculation. Another factor is whether your school incorporates "plus" and "minus" grades on your transcript. Note any differences and decide whether it is something that bears explaining. Also check for errors; no bureaucracy is perfect.

CHAPTER 6

BUILDING YOUR RESUME

CREATING YOUR RESUME

You should always include a resume with your application. This is not an employment resume. Your career services office and the resume services available online are of limited use to you here. The resume is your chance to show what you're all about in a way not provided for in sufficient blank lines on the applications themselves. This is your chance to show leadership, the extent to which you self-financed your application, cultural activities, language proficiencies, and athletic talents. My rules of resume writing for law school applications follow.

Three main rules of resume writing must be incorporated in each of the following sections:

1. Do not refer to yourself in the first person.
2. Use action words in your descriptions.
3. Use past tense to describe positions held in the past, and present tense to describe current duties.

The #1 question I get from clients about resumes is "How long should my resume be?" Only one law school currently dictates a one-page limit. If you have the goods to fill two pages with worthwhile information, then it's perfectly acceptable to do so. However, three pages is only tolerable in very rare cases. Maybe once a year, I'll let someone get away with a 3-page resume. In most cases, if you can't fit it on two pages then you're not using your space wisely. Too much white space and use of a 12-point font is usually the reason for having to go to a second or third page. The resume templates cause a lot of this; don't use a template.

NO HIGH SCHOOL

You will note a common theme here of only listing things that took place **after high school graduation.** Your high school honors, athletics, and awards got you into college; now you need to stand on your college accomplishments. I know, in your head, you might be saying, "Well, that rule doesn't apply to me because I was high school valedictorian/captain of the football team/won a very special award...." To consider yourself special in this regard is a big mistake. Emphasizing high school often unintentionally highlights youth ("she was in high school 3 years ago!"), immaturity ("she thinks this is important?"), lackluster college performance ("she didn't do so well once she moved out from under the watchful eye and mommy and daddy"), and privilege ("she went to that high school?"). Perhaps I'm being cruel, but this is absolutely necessary, because I want to scare you on this point. If you follow my advice on this one point, the cost of this book will have more than paid for itself.

Since you are an aspiring lawyer, you should know that every rule has an exception. Even I have made exceptions for clients whose high school accomplishments add context to their later achievements. For example:

a. Playing as a member of a professional symphony at the age of 16.
b. Olympic-level competitive figure skating to show the import of college hours spent volunteering to teach skating to underprivileged youth.
c. Moving to the U.S. while in high school and learning English as a second language as a teenager, but still graduating high school with honors.
d. If you attended a fancy prep school on full scholarship and your socio-economic circumstances would have otherwise prevented your attendance. If this is the case, make it clear in the descriptive bullet under the school name.

Some of my colleagues maintain that being an Eagle Scout is worth mentioning, but in my mind if you still feel the need to list this accomplishment, your promise of future leadership predicted by such a designation went largely unfulfilled. Again, this is something that got you into college.

Even these examples (listed in a-d) are probably better mentioned in the personal statement than on the resume. By mentioned I mean mentioned, and not the center of the statement.

SUMMARY OF QUALIFICATIONS

This section should only be included on a resume for

people with more than five years of work experience and then only sparingly. The section is helpful if you've had a long professional career in more than one profession. For example, if you're trying to pull together experiences that seem unrelated, demonstrate that throughout all of these jobs you served as a manager of budgets and people. If you decide to incorporate this section, it should include concrete statements of accomplishments ("Supervised budgets exceeding $5 million and up to 17 employees") and not generalities ("History of proven excellence in customer relations"). The reason for this is that general evaluation type statements are more credible when said by an objective third party than by you.

NO OBJECTIVE SECTIONS

Please. Your objective is getting into a certain law school and that's it. Just leave it out.

EDUCATION COMES FIRST

You are applying for professional school. Your educational background is the most important thing and in 95% of cases should be the first section of your resume. If you've been out of school for ten or more years and your undergraduate history is nothing special, I might be ok with it being listed after your professional experience. However, in this case, the professional experience had better be pretty darn impressive and not simply ten years' worth of twenty different secretarial positions.

For the Education section of your resume you should list, in reverse chronological order, the schools you have attended since high school graduation. You do not need to list every school where you took summer school, but should list any school you attended for a significant amount of time.

When presenting information in your resume, think about what the law schools will believe to be most important. Anything that emphasizes academic ability comes before extra-curricular activities. Within that hierarchy, honors are more important than activities, and a thesis is more important than an honor society. When you list activities, leadership and significant involvements in organizations are more important than an organization that appears to be law related but you were only involved in for two months and all you did as part of that involvement was attend a few meetings offering free pizza.

Any font or formatting that is legible and professional looking is fine. The relevant information to include is:

Proper Name of Degree
(Date Conferred/Anticipated Date)
Formal Name of School, City, ST
Major/Minor Information
GPA (if over 3.0)
Honors: (including Dean's List and the semesters or number of semesters total, honor societies, and scholarships)
Activities/Leadership: (list on-campus activities and describe the extent of your involvement)

Study abroad programs should also be listed here, including a description of the length of time you studied abroad, the school name, location, dates, and whether or not you studied the language and culture as part of the experience.

If you wrote a thesis, include the title under the major/minor information.

Refrain from a "Relevant Coursework" section. Law schools will have your transcripts.

EXPERIENCE

Depending upon how much work experience you have, you might choose to call this section any of the following:

Experience
Employment
Professional Employment

You may even break up your employment into "College Employment" and "Professional Employment." If you've had two career tracks and you do not want to appear scattered, you might even want one heading each, such as one for "Teaching Experience" and one heading for "Publishing Experience."

If you had jobs that overlapped with each other, clearly describe the amount of hours worked at each job per week.

For each job, include factual statements of your accomplishments ("assisted in the sale of four homes, resulting in more than $3 million in sales) rather than general conclusions ("learned valuable business skills").

What should be included in this section of your resume?

List all jobs since high school graduation. I don't care how unimpressive you think the job is, it's relevant because it: (a) shows how you chose to spend your time; (b) adds context to your grades and other achievements, even helping to explain why you had a hard time with grades during a certain semester when you had to work full time; (c) demonstrates time management skills (hopefully); (d) shows you weren't a recluse and that you had to deal with other people at work; (e) unglamorous or "menial" jobs build character and demonstrate a lack of snobbery.

Again, exceptions to the "all jobs" rule are rare, but there are a few:

- If you made your money as a professional gambler, you might have second thoughts about sharing it, although in some circumstances it could add character and interest to an application.
- Jobs you held for a very short time probably shouldn't be listed by themselves. Perhaps consider having a section for "Other Employment" or "Freelance Employment" and summarizing the less significant positions. For example: "Also worked 3 hrs/week as a customer service representative at *Best Buy* and *The Gap* in City, ST during fall 2001." Or: "Assisted various event companies with concerts and fundraisers 1-2 weekends a month during holiday and summer breaks 2002-2004."

ACTIVITIES AND COMMUNITY SERVICE

List all activities, honors, and community service since high school graduation. Some notes:

a. For any activities that were campus-related, list them under the appropriate school listing in the Education Section (see above). Reserve a separate heading for anything done outside the confines of the schools you attended after graduation.

b. Don't call it a "Leadership" section if you haven't really been much of a leader. Calling it "leadership" will only point out how little experience you have and won't successfully color the activities you choose to share.

c. If you joined the pre law society or Phi Alpha Delta your last year in school simply to put it on your resume, it will be laughable. At least be able to add a description along the lines of "Joined in Fall 2009 to explore developing interest in law. Attended weekly events, helped coordinate annual Pre Law Panel event, and actively networked with prelaw advisors and professors."

d. Don't assume everyone knows what the "Blue Key Society" is, but do assume everyone knows what "Golden Key Honour Society" is, and please spell it correctly since everyone also knows how it should be spelled.

e. Detail duties, responsibilities, and accomplishments. The point of sharing activities on your resume is to demonstrate your interests and passions and to show that you seriously committed yourself to each. Therefore, stating your duties and accomplishments and the hours you spent per week on each helps to give the reader an indication of the extent of your involvement. It's one thing to list "Member, ABC" and another to list "Member, ABC (2002-2006), actively involved in recruiting 12 new members in 2004 and 14 in 2005, served on committee to orga- nize X event and served as chair of committee when appointed chair became unavailable. 2 hrs/week." Much more impressive, right?

I had a client whose resume was all law. Law and Society major, President of the Pre-Law club, on the Law Journal staff, and an internship at a law firm. I begged her to include a section on her resume about teaching herself to play golf, because otherwise she might have appeared passionless and uninteresting. Law schools can teach you law, but they can't teach you to be well rounded. Showing direction is one thing, but being boring is another.

If you have participated in activities that were outside the confines of a campus environment, you should list them separately from the Education section. In fact, even if your involvements were all campus-related, you might consider listing them separately if there are more than three to list. If you participated in many organizations and can split them up between "Leadership" and "Activities," or "Cultural Activities" and "Peer Education," this might be worth doing, because it highlights that you had certain causes or issues rather than simply joining everything. If you participated in more than one or two community service or volunteer activities, those are probably worth putting in a separate section as well. What you want to avoid is having four headings, each with one listing. All that will accomplish is highlighting how little community service you've done.

SKILLS

Including a "Skills" section can help demonstrate that you are well rounded and accomplished in ways your transcripts and application materials do not reflect.

Do not include computer skills such as "Internet, Word,

Excel." These skills are now simply life skills and not exceptional in any way. If you have been a legal secretary and you are trying to show familiarity with billing and calendaring software, just leave it off your resume. It won't impress anyone and it will be understood from your job description. However, if you have computer programming skills or other technical skills, they should be included.

As Ben Stiller's character Rabbi Jake Schram stated in Keeping the Faith, "Jogging is not a skill." It's an activity and maybe an interest. It's even a hobby, perhaps. It's not a skill.

Other worthwhile examples include:

a. Acrobatic Aviation or even just a pilot's license for those who are less adventurous, but "acrobatic aviation," followed by a description of the training and tricks and years of instruction, sticks with me as a favorite "activity" and "interest" on a client's resume.

b. Completing a Marathon or Triathalon or Team in Training race.

c. Involvement in a non-profit organization, including a church or political group. Although you may choose not to include certain things like religious and political involvement on resumes you'll be sending to employers, law schools will appreciate these associations and interests because they show more about who you are and what is important to you. This information is relevant because it's part of the diversity you bring to the class. The same goes for sexual-orientation. While I understand why applicants may be hesitant to share their involvement in GLBT organizations or their experience campaigning for gay rights issues, I say go for it. It highlights your diversity and the perspective you bring to the law school classroom. Besides, for those who are worried about a law school judging them, I say, "Why would you want to attend a law school that would not welcome and value you?" Test them by being truthful.

d. Anything that shows discipline, maturity, focus, or a sense of humor.

e. Languages are definitely skills worthy of inclusion. Being bi-lingual or multi-lingual is very attractive to law schools. You should state the languages and your degree of proficiency in them. This might include describing your fluency by stating you are a "native speaker," or "completed 4 years of collegiate level study," or "fluent spoken, proficient written," or "intermediate knowledge." No matter how you characterize your language ability, keep two key rules in mind. First, do not oversell yourself. If an admission officer picked up the phone and started talking in Hebrew, would you regret putting a proficiency in Hebrew on your resume? Second, please do not list your fluency in English. Please. It should be a given, since everything else in the application process is in English. If English is a second or third language for you, this should be obvious from the transcripts and essays in your application.

TRAVEL

Seeing the world is a good thing. Showing law schools you've seen the world is a good thing. When can it be a bad thing? Here are some examples:

1. When it sounds more like you come from a privileged family and you tagged along with mommy and daddy on vacations.
2. When it looks like you never took the initiative to travel anywhere on your own.
3. When none of the travel has taken place since high school graduation.

If your travel experience is limited to a college study abroad trip, describe it either under the Education section or under the Travel section, but not in both. If you spent significant time growing up in another country, it is worth mentioning. If you participated in a community service project in a foreign country, you can list it under either Travel or a Community Service section.

If you decide to incorporate a Travel section, list the countries you've visited and if you spent a significant amount of time there, saved up for the trip, concentrated on art museums, religious sites, or trail biking, these are all details worth sharing because they add interest and meaning to the listing and show depth beyond being a simple tourist.

LAST NOTE ON RESUMES:

If you still have 6-12 months before applying to law school, take some time to make an honest assessment of your experiences now that you've seen how they look on paper. Do you your interests seem all over the map with no consistency? Is there something you could continue doing this year that would show growth in that interest? If you've been primarily involved in your fraternity, is there something you could do to show another interest you have, such as a painting class? If your grades and activities are run-of-the mill, could you complete an honors thesis or take on research for a professor that would highlight a sincere academic interest and ability? If you've been working in one profession for years, is there a volunteer activity you could undertake that would show a more clear interest in attending law school? Take time for introspection. It never hurts anyone, and neglecting to do so often leads to laziness and an inflated sense of self. Don't be lazy; be proactive!

CHAPTER 7

PERSONAL STATEMENT

A H – the chapter you've all been waiting for...
A good personal statement adds to the application. It tips the scales in your favor. If someone with your numbers has a possibility of being admitted to a particular school, but not everyone with your numbers is admitted to that school, the major deciding factor is the personal statement. It's your chance to become more than a list of your accomplishments, more than your transcripts, more than your LSAT score. This is your chance to be personable, likeable, and impressive without being arrogant, and to generally give the impression that you'd be a great asset to their school and alumni base.

You must be more than your transcripts, resume, and LORs. The personal statement is the "more." It's what makes you a person and not just a number. Being likeable and impressive makes an admission officer want to go to bat for you. This is your one and only chance to tell a law school what it wouldn't otherwise know about you. Don't blow it!

The Personal Statement is the part of the application that makes each applicant the most nervous. I could, and will, write an entire book on how to create effective law school personal statements that boost your chances of acceptance. I'm always amazed at law school admission books that fail to dedicate significant space to this part of the application. I'm even more amazed at how uniformly terrible and cliché the published "sample" personal statements are in each of these books. I urge you not to read them, even though I know you will read them anyway. It's like watching the aftermath of a car accident; you know it's useless to look and will only slow you down, but you look anyway. In this chapter, I describe why the personal statement is so important and how to use this great opportunity to your advantage.

What Are Law Schools Looking for in a Personal Statement?

There are certain things a law school wants to be assured of: maturity despite youth; commitment to the study of law despite lacking a specific career aspiration; ability to succeed in a rigorous environment; independent thinking skills; and feeling a duty greater than simple self-interest. A good personal statement uses none of these phrases, but tells a story that convinces the readers to come to the conclusions on their own.

A good personal statement is interesting to read without needing to rely on shock value. It has a conversational rather than academic tone; it's not there to show how many big words you know. Lawyers need to write in clear sentences. Start now.

As Director of Admissions for law schools, I would groan, roll my eyes, and write sarcastic comments on personal statements hinting of the following:

- Arrogance and elitism.
- A purported drive to serve others and to heal the world and be a public interest lawyer when there's

little community service in the person's background to back it up.

- Repeating a resume.
- Providing lots of conclusions with few facts to back them up, for example, starting a sentence with, "My strong work ethic…" and then not really showing anything remarkable about your work ethic.
- Not being specific enough and talking around issues ("I had a rough time but overcame obstacles") without giving details so that the readers can evaluate for themselves whether the feat was impressive.
- Spelling errors.
- Excessive use of passive voice.
- Attempting to write a treatise on the importance of law in society.

There is a misconception that personal statements must be about overcoming paralysis or poverty. It's completely acceptable for someone who grew up with plenty of everything to want to attend law school. Just show some perspective and that you've done something meaningful with your life. Many people remember their clever undergraduate essay about contemplating the lumps of peanut butter and think they should repeat that. Please don't. Remember, we're going for maturity here.

Generally, I urge people to stay away from high school unless there's a really good reason to talk about it, such as a traumatic event that created the necessity for you to self-finance college or remain close to home, or something that shows growth, maturity, and overcoming obstacles. High school sports should never be mentioned, nor should high school mock trial competitions. This is the stuff that got you into college. What have you done to get yourself into law school? What you did while living under your parents' roof as a teenager is not going to impress anyone at this time in your life. A notable exception is the 18 year-old college graduate applying to law school.

SECRETS TO A SUCCESSFUL PERSONAL STATEMENT

Use Your Own Voice.

This is about the tone of your essay.

The point of the personal statement is for the reader to like you and to want to pass you in the halls every day for the next three years, so keep that in mind as you write the very first draft. It's important to be likeable and to create the impression that you will be an alumnus who will reflect well upon the law school (without taking yourself too seriously, of course).

Don't try to sound how you *think* a personal statement should sound, and certainly don't try to write one of those cheesy personal statements you saw in some book of sample law school personal statements. I always advise my clients to attempt the first draft as though they are speaking the words instead of writing them. Think of that first draft as a journal entry or a written conversation. Take the pressure off yourself and stay away from clever introductions, conclusions, and literary motifs. Just think about the heart of the story as you're starting out.

This is not an academic paper, and if you try to write how you expect lawyers write, using many big words, you'll just make a fool of yourself. A good personal statement allows the reader to get to know **you** and to like **you**, and this means taking a conversational tone. A successful personal statement lets the reader get to know the writer. This means writing about **yourself** and not about the time you had lunch with "Mary" during a one-time visit to a homeless shelter and your resulting epiphany about the effects of poverty.

Surprise the Reader

By the time someone reads your personal statement, she will already know your GPA, LSAT, work history, honors, awards, activities, and more. What might that person assume about you from this information? Think critically about yourself.

Will your transcripts make you look lazy? If so, tell a story that shows how hard working and focused you are. Likewise, if your transcripts show you're a near-perfect student, and you have the LORs and resume to back it up, share something surprising in the personal statement by getting personal. Show them you're more than what they think you are. If you graduated college in three years and you're 20, demonstrate maturity. If you went to fancy private schools, recount tales of how you competed for scholarships and worked as a hostess to pay your bills. If you appear to be the "typical" sorority girl or jock, share your love of reading or museums.

However, this approach only works if the story you're telling is true, because those of us who have read tens of thousands of personal statements can spot the B.S. quickly. Be real. Don't apologize for not having done more; just show the purpose behind the decisions you've made. It's ok to admit to mistakes. Just demonstrate the growth you experienced as a result.

Avoid Conclusions

A good personal statement never says, "I always wanted to be a lawyer," or "I overcame obstacles," or "I never quit in the face of adversity." Rather, it tells a story that convinces the reader to come to these conclusions on his or her own. How do you do this? By providing facts and telling a true story that shows the conclusion you're trying to prove. This is how you succeed on law school exams as well, and the best way for a lawyer to make an effective argument is to use the facts of the case; start with your law school personal statement.

One of my pet peeves when I was reviewing law school applications as director of admissions was reading statements like, "I overcame obstacles" and then not really learning what those obstacles were. I am more likely to assume this is an overstatement than to give anyone the benefit of the doubt, especially when confronted with more compelling stories in the other files on my desk.

If part of your strategy is to show you are more of an academic than your transcripts might demonstrate, this is the time to share that you held two jobs in college and went to a professor's office hours weekly to catch up with the grad students enrolled in the 500 level course, and how you worked like crazy to earn that B- and it was one of your best accomplishments. (Plus, you have the opportunity to build upon this by asking that professor to write a LOR). If you provide persuasive facts to add credibility to your assertions, the reader will make the right conclusion naturally.

Consider Your Content

Some law school applicants mistakenly believe that the goal of the personal statement is to write something so memorable that it will be talked about all year. This really only happens in two cases: (1) when an essay is so ridiculous that it becomes a joke among admission committee members; and (2) when an applicant's life story is so compelling and impressive that it's not an essay you could try to write, but rather happens organically, because the content is so unique. Obviously, we'd all like to avoid situation #1 and be situation #2, but situation #1 is more within your control. Removing the goal of standing out will make it much easier for you to begin writing.

The goal is to present a picture of yourself as someone who is ready for law school. You do not want to do this by directly addressing why you are ready for law school, but rather by telling a story that shows that you are a thinking person, someone who has experienced life, understands something about how the world works, and who brings something to the table that adds to a law school's class. You can do this by sharing a story about how your family background taught you the importance of working hard for what you want, or how running a student organization taught you to deal with difficult situations, or pretty much any story that illustrates the qualities you are trying to share.

However, some topics have become trite and overused, including:

a. The injured athlete story, "It was difficult to leave the team after I worked so hard for so many years…";

b. The typical study abroad story, "I learned to drive on the wrong side and to use chopsticks…";

c. Current historical events, "Obama's rise to the presidency inspires me.";

d. High school events, "In high school, I was a championship softball player and earned 6 AP credits. High school can be appropriate to mention if there's a specific episode that proves a point you're trying to make, such as "My parents divorced during my junior year of high school, and suddenly I learned I would have to bear the cost of college myself. As a result, I worked 30 hours a week during my freshman year…");

e. The "Childhood Dream" story. Stay away from writing about your parents praising you for negotiating a later bedtime at age four and from stating that your desire to become a lawyer began with Matlock/LA Law/Law and Order/Ally McBeal/The Practice, or watching the O.J. trial.

You don't have to apologize for having a privileged life, just show what does make you interesting, different, or remarkable. Some of my clients have distinguished themselves in non-traditional ways by doing things they never even considered mentioning in their law school personal statements. One has a huge readership on her crafts blog, and yes, she is attending a top-ten school. Another ran an on-line gaming community, again, he is attending a top-ten school. Don't underestimate what you have going for you, and don't take yourself too seriously.

One last bit of advice on the choice of topic: stay away from anything that will make you appear to be high maintenance, such as recounting the time you fought the dean of students about the professor who had a grudge against you because you were late to her class once.

Use Your Words Wisely

Spell correctly.
Punctuate correctly.

Don't use 10 words when 3 will do. (Sorry if I'm paraphrasing Ocean's 11 here).

Think about what you're writing. There is no reason to start with, "My name is…" when your name is at the top of the paper. Refrain from repeating things that the reader will already know about you (job descriptions, awards won, etc.).

Don't mention a law school's name unless you're going to say something specific and meaningful about the school.

Refrain from adding content just because a school says a personal statement can be up to four pages. You don't get bonus points for additional words. You get bonus points for being succinct.

Trust Your Judgment

It's a good idea to have another set of eyes on your personal statement before you submit it. After you look at something a hundred times, it's hard to spot the errors yourself. However, be careful about passing your essay around to lawyers, English professors, parents, and friends. A personal statement is such a different type of writing, and its purpose is so specific, that unless someone has had experience making law school admission decisions, they probably have only read one personal statement in their lives, their own.

It's probably worth the investment to hire a web-based editing service. Some charge only $0.13 a word, and if it saves you from making a careless mistake, it was worth every penny and more.

Friends, parents, and attorneys probably expect that you should spend your essay talking about your public speaking skills, how your friends always seek your advice, and the important role lawyers hold in society. Be strong enough to decide against taking certain advice. Instead, consider seeking the advice of a pre-law advisor or a professor. Another option is to hire a law school admission consultant.

Three Things to Avoid Putting in a Personal Statement

1. **Titles**.

   Just put your name, LSAC# and the words "Personal Statement" in the header. No titles.

2. **Opening or Closing Quotes of Famous People**.

   You have only 500-1000 words to convince a law school to admit you. Don't waste your personal statement on anything not personal to you. If you need more reasons: (1) eyes skip right over a quote; (2) it always seems right out of a high school English paper; and (3) it's cheesy in absolutely every circumstance. I once had a Hindu client start his personal statement draft with a quote from the Old Testament. Needless to say, I edited that part out.

3. **Pleas for Acceptance**.

   Your personal statement should convince the reader to admit you based on the strength of your experiences and perspective. No begging at the end. None of this, "I truly hope for the opportunity to prove myself" nonsense. It didn't work for Tatiana on American Idol. You made fun of her for pleading to the camera, right? It made her seem crazy, right? So, why on earth would you try it when applying for professional school?

5 WORDS & PHRASES THAT MAKE ME CRINGE IN PERSONAL STATEMENTS:

1. "**Personally**…" It's a personal statement. Of course everything you say is your own personal opinion. If it's not, you're doing something wrong.

2. "**In conclusion**…" Blech! Just conclude, don't announce that you're concluding.

3. "**I believe**..." It doesn't matter what you believe about your ability to succeed in law school or what you believe is important in your application. The fact that you believe it is immaterial. Just state the facts so that the reader independently concludes that he or she believes whatever you're trying to prove.

4. "**Unique**..." Very few things in this world are "unique," especially the use of the word unique.

5. "**Firsthand experience**..." What is a secondhand experience and why would anyone write about it? Of course your experiences are "firsthand."

DECIDING WHAT TO WRITE ABOUT

I don't believe in sample personal statements, and I refuse to offer them to my clients. While many of my clients receive handwritten notes about their personal statements from the deans of the law schools where they are admitted, I would not want to share these essays because there is a singular reason they are effective in the admissions process. Each is personal to the person writing it; no two are the same.

However, I do understand the craving law school applicants have for reading other people's personal statements, since the task appears so daunting. Rather than succumb to your unproductive desires, I will share four case studies with you.

I do not expect any of these case studies to fit perfectly with anyone else's story or to provide the one and only answer to the question of what to write your personal statement about. Instead, I offer these case studies as examples for picking themes that will help you in the admission process and add that "more" to your application.

Case Study #1

I am three years out of college and I've held a few jobs. I worked as a mortgage broker's assistant, then as a publishing assistant, then sold classified ads for an online magazine. What do I write my personal statement about?

For those of you a few years out of college who have held 2-3 jobs that weren't promotions within the same company or industry, then applying to law school can appear insincere. It can look like you're floundering and still trying to find yourself. When objectively analyzing your resume, consider the impact of this trend and consider ways to overcome it, perhaps by emphasizing a volunteer position, or thinking about ways the jobs actually have more in common with each other than meets the eye, or considering how each job has actually allowed you to come closer to your conclusion that law school is the right next step for you. You might also consider this theme by sharing a story from your personal life about the impact a lawyer had on your family's situation, even if the impact was negative.

Case Study #2

I am a law and society major, president of the pre-law club, and an editor on the pre-law journal. I also worked as a legal

assistant for a local attorney this year. How do I discuss this in
my personal statement without repeating my resume?

You have two choices. Discuss a particular story from one of these experiences that shows growth, or show a completely different side of yourself that will show you are, despite what the rest of your application suggests, a well rounded person. You could write about the time you stood up to the other PAD officers on an ethical issue, or how the most difficult and surprising event only confirmed your desire to become an attorney. The other option might include sharing how you taught yourself to speak Spanish, why you volunteer at the film festival every year, or your experience helping a friend through a difficult situation.

Case Study #3

I don't have any extra curricular activities or dean's list honors
or anything like that. I went to a state school and did ok, but I
worked 25-30 hours a week throughout to pay my own bills. My
jobs weren't very exciting. I tended bar mostly. How do I make
myself stand out?

First of all, you have two things going for you, financial self-reliance and an ability to multi-task. Your accomplishments didn't come cheap; you probably appreciate your degree more because you were paying for it. These themes go a long way in law school admissions, and you probably met some interesting characters and learned some life lessons in the process. An ability to relate to people from different backgrounds is an important trait for an attorney to demonstrate. Don't sell yourself short or apologize for what you have not done. Instead, tell a story that shows an appreciation for the realities of life.

Case Study #4

> *I've worked in IT for twelve years. The work is mostly outsourced to India now and, to be frank, I need a new profession. How do I make this less obvious in my law school applications, and how do I deal with my low Computer Information Systems GPA from fifteen years ago?*

If you've worked on any projects that interfaced with law, that might help you provide a good tie-in to a natural move to law school. If not, have you done any volunteer work that shows your interest in other things? Or, if you freelanced and worked for yourself, can you repackage your experience as general "how to run a business" experience and perhaps add in any times that knowing the law would have been helpful to you in running your business? Another way to go might be to think about your family situation and show another side of yourself that law schools won't know about from reviewing your resume. Emphasize life lessons and maturity. Demonstrate that you know what you're getting yourself into with the financial and time investment of returning to school.

SCHOOL-SPECIFIC PERSONAL STATEMENTS

Unless a school specifically asks you to address reasons for applying to that school, you do not have to mention a school's name in your personal statement. However, there may be reasons for doing so. The most important one is that it shows the law school that you have real reasons for applying and would seriously consider attending, therefore making the school's yield bet pay off in deciding to send you an acceptance letter (or, more commonly, an acceptance email). However, most of my law school admission consulting clients struggle to state the reasons they are applying to a certain law school. I want to offer some hints and tricks in this regard, because sometimes law schools just don't seem to be that different from one another, especially when they are ranked similarly.

> "Yield" is a law school's number of accepted students versus students who eventually matriculate. This is what US News refers to as "acceptance rate" in its rankings. Therefore, to "protect the yield," schools will waitlist, hold, and flat-out deny applicants whose numbers are within range or high when the school does not believe there is a strong likelihood of attendance. Mentioning a school in your personal statement helps demonstrate sincere interest in attending.

Here are some tips:

a. Never just plug a school's name into a fill-in-the-blank statement. If you could change the school and still say the same thing, your statement isn't specific enough to help you. For example:

    "X Law School boasts an excellent faculty and several clinical experiences that provide hands-on learning."
    "The reputation of X Law School leads me to apply."

b. Don't say you love their Environmental Law program if nothing in your application supports your interest in Environmental Law. Just because they have a brochure about it doesn't mean it should be your reason for applying.

c. Don't pick a study abroad program as your reason; you can do almost any ABA school's study abroad summer program and transfer the credits.

d. Don't list reasons that could be applied to any law school equally like 'esteemed faculty' or 'national reputation' or 'bar passage rate.' Be specific.

e. If you're applying part-time, tell them why. Otherwise, they'll think you're just using the part time program to be admitted through the "back door."

f. Location is very important. If your background screams "Boston!" you should provide a reason for applying to a law school in San Diego. Having family nearby or a fiancé with a job there will absolutely help allay any concerns about yield that a school might have if you are a candidate whose decision could easily go either way.

BREVITY RULES

Do what a school wants you to do. If the school's directions say two pages, don't play with the margins and spacing and font to get it to fit. I've never seen a personal statement of any length that I couldn't easily cut down to two pages, 500, or even 250 words. If you think an exception should be made to the length restriction simply because you're more brilliant than anyone else, you're delusional. If you can't edit your work and decide between essential and superfluous words and ideas, you're actually the opposite of brilliant. Cutting a personal statement to size shouldn't mean sacrificing content; it should require you to really think about your message and what is essential to include for you to prove that message. Many of my clients are actually so thrilled with the shorter versions of their essays that they choose to use those versions even for schools that allow longer essays.

CHAPTER 8

OPTIONAL ESSAYS

MANY schools are giving applicants the opportunity to submit a secondary essay with their applications. Sometimes a school calls this a "Diversity Statement" and sometimes it's referred to as an "Optional Essay." Check a school's website and application to see whether it's given as an option. If it is, and if the topic applies to your situation, I highly recommend doing it. This provides another opportunity to show something new about yourself and to express your interest in the law school. Some common topics include what I will refer to as the Diversity Statement, the Why X Law School statement, the Career Statement, and the Unique Contributions statement (discussed more in depth below).

I know it just seems like more work, but if you're faced with an optional essay topic that applies to you, stop bitching and just do it. Would you turn down a second interview with an employer? Not if you were interested in the job. The optional essay is the same thing. If you're not interested in showing a school more of what you've got, you're probably not seriously interested in the school and you should rethink your reasons for applying.

SHOULD YOU WRITE THE
OPTIONAL ESSAY?

Do it *if* it applies to you and would not repeat your personal statement. If the topic does not apply to you, if you do not bring multi-cultural, ethnic, religious, socio-economic or other diversity to the table, do not write the essay. Please do not attempt the "My best friend is gay" essay or the "through my work at Starbucks, I learned to work with all kinds of people" essay. If you feel yourself reaching, the law schools will also feel you reaching. Only submit an optional essay if it adds to the quality of your application; don't let it bring everything else down.

> You do not have to be an underrepresented minority to be considered diverse. One of my Korean-American clients did not want to write a diversity statement because she argued that Asian Americans were actually overrepresented in law school. However, I encouraged her to write a diversity statement about her study abroad experience in Japan and the perspective it lent her given the history of the two cultures and lingering resentment. It turned out to be a beautiful and insightful essay about cultural awareness and overcoming personal bias.

If the topic of your optional essay would repeat your personal statement, consider submitting your personal statement as your optional essay and writing a new personal statement for that school.

If you do write the optional essay, stay within the confines of what you are being asked, including all word and page limits provided. Following directions is part of the test. After all, if a judge says to keep your trial brief to five pages you'd be an idiot to send her six pages.

THE DIVERSITY STATEMENT

Why is diversity so important to law schools? Because there's so much of it in society and not enough of it in law schools. The biggest problem I see with diverse applicants is that diversity is often under recognized and misdiagnosed. What I mean by this is that people with diversity are usually unable to recognize it in themselves or reluctant to express it because they've worked so hard to assimilate or because it's painful to consider themselves as different from others.

An example of this is the person who was raised by a single mother who came to the U.S. from another country and worked two low-wage jobs to make sure the daughter could attend private schools. Another example would be the person who is African-American but doesn't feel comfortable doing more than checking off a box because his parents are professionals. I believe an argument can be made that an African-American man in this country faces prejudice, whether blatant or latent, to some extent, no matter how educated. Both of these individuals bring diversity and unique cultural perspectives to the table, and each should write a diversity statement.

Here are some additional diversity characteristics worth sharing:

1. Language and cultural literacy that will help you to represent people who often find it difficult to traverse American society.
2. Being the first in your family to go to college.
3. Military service.

4. Saving for college by working during high school and college and the lessons this taught you.

5. Living overseas during your formative years and coming to the U.S. from another country as a child or teenager.

6. Coming from a household where you or others were physically abused.

7. How your experience coming out of the closet led you to help others to do the same.

8. Your experiences gaining respect in the business world while wearing a veil or turban.

9. Having a child during high school or college and earning your undergraduate degree while supporting a family.

10. Experiencing poverty, including reliance upon public assistance and charities.

The whole point of diversity is that it isn't just checking off a box. This list is just a sample of what can be considered diverse for purposes of an optional essay. Everyone is different, and every story is different. The point is that if you believe you have something compelling to share in this regard, you should do so. If you do not, don't apologize for it. Be thankful for your blessings and that you've presented yourself in the best possible light in each part of the application that did apply to you. For all of the talk about overcoming obstacles, remember that the essays about overcoming paralysis and poverty are moving because the stories themselves are so rare. Share your story and never apologize for not having someone else's story to share. It's what you've done with what you were given that matters, in law school and in life.

The "Why X Law School" Statement

Unless you're already living in or have ties to the city where the law school is based, this question might throw you for a loop. After all, most law schools have the same brochure text. Every school's website discusses its hands-on approach to law and the reputation of its faculty. The key to successfully answering this question is to be specific about the school and your experiences.

Location is always a winner. If you have family in the area or if you've lived there before, you should mention it, since it would be more likely that you'd make the move there for law school.

> Never "pick a major" going into law school unless your personal and work experience truly supports it. Most people end up picking an area of specialization depending upon who hires them, and most law school applicants are too idealistic to accept that that's the case. You're more likely to be satisfied with your career if you're open minded about this now.

In addition to geography, think about things you've studied or researched in the past. Does the school have any clinics, journals, or faculty members who published in these areas? Discuss how you would continue to explore these topics in law school, and how the law school is uniquely situated to encourage that endeavor. This lets you highlight something about you that might not be evident from your application, and allows you to expand upon something mentioned in a letter of recommendation so you can build a theme across your application and ensure consistency throughout your materials.

Another idea is to look through the faculty biographies. Does anyone speak your language, literally or figuratively? Are there three professors who spent significant time in Asia (just like you!) or two professors who used to work for the SEC (which is where you hope to work!)? Mentioning this shows you've done your research about the school while also demonstrating that you have a serious interest in law that you hope to explore further.

It is also helpful to mention strong reviews from students and alumni, whether in personal conversations with people you know, who should be mentioned by name, or through online or published resources including a school's survey results that might be posted on its website.

When a law school boasts about its interdisciplinary approach to education and the ability to take classes in another graduate program, this helps develop content for the "Why X Law School" essay. Beware, however, that this topic only has credibility if you have something specific you hope to study or you have studied in this manner in the past. The opportunity to explore lots of different areas of law is always worth mentioning if you have several areas of law that interest you at this point. It's a way to show you've researched the breadth of courses offered and the wide expertise of the faculty.

Class size, programs that bring faculty and students together, academic support above and beyond the ordinary, and diversity of the student body as demonstrated by specific statistics and/or student organizations are also good aspects to mention. Anything that shows you've done your research will help your essay. When reviewing applications, it was always fun for me to have brochure text that I wrote quoted back to me in an essay. In reality, however, I wanted to know that an applicant was capable of delving further and evaluating the substantive information available about my school.

Things you should NOT include in a "Why X Law School" essay:

1. Mentioning an area of concentration in which you have no previous experience or exposure.
2. Interest in a law school solely because of its study abroad program. Generally, you can do any school's summer study abroad program so you wouldn't have to go to that law school to participate.
3. Rankings. The exception to this rule would be ranking in your particular (well supported by experience and research) area of specialization.

The Career Statement

Where do you hope to be in ten years? Why do you want to be a lawyer? What are your goals upon obtaining your law degree? Some iteration of these questions is often asked in the personal statement prompt and/or in an optional essay topic. First, remember that it's perfectly ok (and arguably more credible and mature) to say that you have no idea what kind of law you plan to practice, but that law is a good fit for you because of certain strengths and personality characteristics and you enjoy writing, research, and crafting arguments (as demonstrated by X, Y and Z, of course).

Another way to go would be to discuss the particular community and how you hope to contribute to the community surrounding the law school, or even to a community far away if that law school offers something you can't get at your home-town law school. What kind of member of the bar will you be? How will you help others and give back?

What is important to you in your career? Working for yourself? Learning from others? Finding a mentor? Mastering one thing or being situated to help a few clients with lots of issues? Do you have experience with family law, contract law, employment law, or something personal you learned that shows you what you might enjoy doing? All of these are fair game for this essay.

The "Unique Contributions" Statement

Sometimes a school's optional essay will give a more open ended prompt, asking you to describe unique contributions you would make to the law school environment. This is an opportunity to share diversity characteristics, but does keep the door open for non-diversity related subject matter.

Examples of potential topics for this essay include:

1. Speaking another language
2. Experience starting a nonprofit or undergraduate organization
3. Connections with local law firms or agencies
4. Significant research conducted on a topic that coincides with one of the school's law journals
5. Experience as a tutor will enable you to help others through the school's academic achievement program

The important thing is to avoid repeating your personal statement. If a school wants only a 500 word personal statement, you might consider taking part of what you've removed from the longer version of that essay and using it as a basis for this optional essay prompt. Another option would be to reserve that story in the event that you are invited to apply for a scholarship and submit an additional essay.

CHAPTER 9

ADDENDA – AN OPPORTUNITY TO EXPLAIN WEAKNESSES

SUBMITTING an addendum to a law school application is a way to explain something the schools might perceive as a weakness and/or provide context to a certain answer you provided on an application.

There are several typical subjects that should be addressed this way, and the most popular are discussed below. No matter the reason for the addendum, some rules apply universally:

1. **Be brief**. A paragraph on each issue should be plenty if you choose your words carefully.
2. **Resolve the issue**. Demonstrate that whatever *was* a problem is no longer a problem.
3. **Be candid**. It's very obvious when details are glossed over. Your explanation will carry more weight if you share all of the vital details.
4. **Filter yourself**. Yes, you may need to share more personal information than you would share on a job interview, but be careful to avoid a list of personal issues so you don't appear troubled, high maintenance, or unwilling to take responsibility.

When considering whether to include an addendum, I urge people to stay away from anything that will make them appear to be high maintenance or complainers in general. Law school faculty and staff won't want to touch you with a ten-foot pole.

EXPLAINING MULTIPLE LSAT SCORES

There are situations regarding multiple LSAT scores that may need to be explained to schools. The important thing about these explanations is to keep them brief, professional, and to-the-point. What you ate for breakfast is not important, nor is the fight you got into with your roommate about the video game tournament keeping you awake. What is important to point out?

1. **Illness**. Not a cold. Seriously. Will you ask a judge for an extension because of a cold? Not if you want to keep practicing law. But vomiting during the exam is worth mentioning (just not graphically, please).

2. **Unreasonable exam conditions**. If they were extraordinarily unreasonable, you should immediately write to LSAC and explain the conditions. They might offer to send a letter with your score about the conditions, but most likely they'll just give you the option of cancelling your score. This letter will not be very helpful, but might add credibility to your claim of being unreasonably distracted throughout the exam.

3. **Significant Score Change**. If you increase your LSAT score by 4 points or more, some kind of explanation is probably warranted.

    If your score actually decreases more than 1-2

points on a subsequent attempt, this should be explained. If your second (or third) score is within 1-3 points of the previous score, perhaps you shouldn't submit any explanation because it's within the same score band of three points and is probably the right score for you, like it or not. If all you can say is that you wish you had done better, you're not adding anything of substance to your application.

Simply cancelling an LSAT score is not worth explaining in an addendum. It's not a mark against you, and it isn't factored into the process. I very rarely counsel an applicant to explain a score cancellation.

UNDERGRADUATE TRANSCRIPTS

Some issues you might want to consider explaining about your transcripts include:

- Inconsistency between school GPA and LSAC GPA. If you repeated courses and performed well in them the second time, this would be worth mentioning.
- An upward trend in grades might be worth explaining. The good news is that the Academic Summary Report is designed to make these trends obvious. Some obvious reasons include slacking off or having too much fun your freshman year. That can probably go without explanation. Same with starting pre-med. Schools will see that on your transcripts. However, if there's a compelling reason (working full time, a death in the family, battling illness, etc.), it would be worth mentioning. The key to any excuse related addendum

is to show that these factors were temporary and have been resolved; you want to assure the law school these factors will not negatively impact your performance in law school.

- The downward trend is more difficult. Factors worth mentioning include increased work hours due to taking on more financial responsibility, moving home to take care of a family member, suffering a death in the family, and an illness that has since been resolved.

If you can provide factual support demonstrating the point you're trying to make, you should do so. For example, if you're trying to argue that your outdated UGPA is not indicative of your potential to perform in a rigorous academic environment, mention courses you've taken toward certifications or in graduate school, and/or any published research or articles.

Academic Probation

This is one of the things you will need to report to law school. You'll want to gather the dates and semesters of the probation. It's important to share a little bit about any contributing factors, and to show you turned yourself around after that.

Moral Character and Fitness Issues

These are the issues that my former assistant director of admissions liked to call "sticky-wickets." First, you need to read the question being asked very carefully to determine whether it applies to you. Each law school words these questions very differently. You don't want to be evasive; you want to err on the side of candor because later, when you are hopefully applying for admission to a state's bar, you do not want to be accused of hiding information on your law school application.

A lot of people have issues to report under this section of the application. The really troublesome things are those having to do with violence, dishonesty, and substance abuse. Obviously, you're considering entering a profession where things like trust and veracity are valued highly; you'll be handling people's money and exerting considerable influence over their lives. It's absolutely ok to have a blemished past; no one expects you to be perfect. However, if you have incidents to report, you need to handle them with grace and fortitude.

How do these factors impact your law school application? In most cases, checking off a "yes" box means that members of the admission committee will review your file even if your numbers are within presumptive admit range and the director or dean of admissions has the authority to admit others in your LSAT/GPA range. It will usually take longer to review your application, and it will make your admission results more unpredictable.

ACADEMIC DISHONESTY & HONOR CODE VIOLATIONS

Law schools take issues like plagiarism and cheating very seriously. Having these incidents in your recent past might effectively bar you from admission to law school. These are obstacles that are hard to overcome. A hazing incident from your sorority can probably be explained in a way that law schools will put it in context and see that it doesn't define you. Cheating might not be automatic disqualification if you show you were part of a group project and did not know that a group member engaged in this conduct, that you were immediately honest about it as soon as you learned of it, and you faced the music. Facing the music is important, and this is a time to take personal responsibility. Blaming others, or even appearing to blame others (such as an unreasonable professor and/or academic pressure to perform) will not get you anywhere.

Minor in Possession Tickets

A minor in possession or underage drinking ticket is not by itself going to negatively impact your chances of admission to law school. Include the date, your age at the time, and the location. You might provide context about the circumstances, particularly if you were not actually caught with the beer but you were in a room where underage individuals were drinking. You should emphasize that this was a long time ago, and/or only a week before your 21st birthday, and that you completed all requirements of the ticket (including an alcohol education class, when applicable). That's really all there is to it. Having more than one ticket makes things more complicated, but if both were several years ago and you can demonstrate growth and maturity since that time, this wouldn't cause the law schools to express great concern over the merits of your application.

Speeding Tickets

Some schools ask about speeding tickets. While this seems stupid to many of us, speeding tickets are not going to keep you out of law school. Four might be funny, but if you provide the dates, fines paid, locations, and offenses (going 45 in a 35 MPH zone), you're probably going to get through unscathed. Problematic issues might arise if you demonstrate a habit of driving dangerously, endangering the lives of others, and driving under the influence more than once and not demonstrating that you learned your lesson after the first occurrence.

ARRESTS & CONVICTIONS

Let me preface this by saying that I've worked with law school applicants who have served time in jail and are still admitted to law school. So, while the road might be uphill, it's not a dead end at the start of the race. A school may ask whether you've been arrested, charged, convicted, or only whether you've been convicted. Be careful about asking the law schools about how you should respond; they will tell you every time that you should disclose everything. Remember that the schools are not looking out for your best interests.

If you have any questions about how to approach these issues on law school applications, it's worth a one-hour consultation with an attorney who specializes in representing other lawyers on moral character and fitness issues in front of the state's bar where you hope to practice. If you have any question whatsoever as to whether your criminal history would preclude you from practicing law, you should contact the state bar and an attorney in the state where you hope to practice law. The time and effort would prove worthwhile before spending thousands applying to law school. It would also give you some peace of mind going forward.

If you do check the "yes" box on this question, you'll want to use the addendum to show maturity, growth, remorse, and that the experience changed you and that it should not label you or limit your potential going forward in life. The way to do this is by providing facts that show this, as opposed to including general statements and conclusions to this effect. Make sure to include the facts (dates, charges, circumstances, etc.) and show how you've put this behind you, how it has impacted your decisions since that time, and why the underlying issues are no longer a problem at this point in your life. The key word is distance. Show that you've put some serious miles between the former you and the current you.

CHAPTER 10

SUBMITTING APPLICATIONS

I T seems so easy, right? You fill out the Common Information form on LSAC.org and let it fill out your applications. You check a few boxes, fill in a few blanks, and press "submit." It's not always quite so simple, and I find many mistakes when reviewing applications before they are submitted. Here are some checklist items for filling out the applications so you don't have a "Uh, Oh!" or "Oh #$@(!" moment after pressing "Submit."

Application Checklist:

1. Follow directions without exception.
2. Find out whether a school requires a Dean's Certificate letter, and if it does, find out where to get the form and the appropriate person to return it to the law school.
3. Pay attention to whether a school wants you to list things in chronological order or reverse chronological order.
4. If a school asks you to list activities or jobs on blank lines, do it. Don't just put "See Resume" in the space provided unless a school specifically states that it's ok to do so.

5. Print out the application and check it on paper.

6. Ask someone else to review the printout.

7. Double-check your address and email information. Make sure you checked either "yes" or "no" on every applicable box.

8. Be certain you are attaching the correct version of the essay(s). If a school doesn't have the personal statement and/or optional essay instructions on the application itself, check the school's website carefully. It's very important to follow the instructions in terms of length, font, and the question being asked. Everything has to be right.

9. Be very, very careful about the things you attach electronically. Turn off the track changes feature and make sure all notes and highlights have been removed.

10. Don't submit a four-page personal statement when three will do. Especially when a school has a three-page limit.

11. If you're not sure, don't guess. Call the school's admission office and ask. If you do something wrong, they may consider your application incomplete and fail to review it.

12. Ask yourself, "Why am I submitting this application right this minute?" If it's late at night, you're exhausted, or feeling hurried, don't submit it. One day isn't going to make a difference, but one mistake might. Wait one day and review it after sleep and a fresh cup of coffee.

Practicing law is all about the details. Start now.

Common Questions about Submitting Applications

Q: Can I submit applications even though LSAC hasn't received and processed my letters of recommendation yet?

A: YES

Q. Should I put my name and LSAC Account number on each attachment to my application?

A. YES

Q. Should I check each school's web site for the application requirements instead of relying on the LSDAS online application?

A. YES

Q. Should I include a creative title on my personal statement?

A. NO

Common Mistakes in Law School Applications

1. Sending School A's personal statement to School B.
2. Spelling errors.
3. Incorrect dates on employment positions.
4. Playing with margins and fonts instead of really taking the time to analyze whether each word in your essay is necessary for its effectiveness.
5. Don't fill in the blanks with junk. If you have no academic honors, don't fake any; just leave the lines blank. The same with activities. It's ok if you can't fill in every blank. Reaching to come up with something

looks desperate, as does listing something as both an extracurricular activity *and* a job.

Your application is the "package" that represents you to a law school. This framework allows you to show your strengths. Use it fully and use it well. It's not just a form, it's the first thing a law school will see and it's what represents you to the school. It matters.

CHAPTER 11

SELECTING SCHOOLS

A client, we'll call him Sam, wanted to attend a top 25 Law School and was unwilling to budge from his goal no matter what I said to enlighten him about other possibilities. He got into one part-time and so decided to wait a year and retake the LSAT. The following year, he got into the same school but full time and chose that school over others closer to his home that offered him generous scholarships. Then, during his first semester at the "top" school, he called me:

"Ann! Do you remember two years ago you said to me, 'US News' Top 25 isn't necessarily [Sam's] Top 25'?"

It sounded like something I would say.

"Well, I'm here full time at this 'top' law school and I'm calling to say you were right and I'm withdrawing. I called [my home-town] law school and they said they'd still offer me the scholarship if I apply for next fall. That's my new strategy! I don't want to be in debt to impress everyone else with what law school I went to. I finally woke up!"

Sam's decision wouldn't be right for everyone, but

considering his goals, ties to home, and absolutely hatred of the idea of taking on any debt whatsoever, he felt this was the right option for him.

The reputation of your school is important, yes, but no one is really choosing New York Law School over New York University, even with a full scholarship. In that respect, rankings matter. However, between this year's #21 and this year's #15, you shouldn't automatically choose #15. First of all, the schools could flip flop in the ranking next year. For example, the top 30 schools don't change much over time. However, if you limit yourself by applying only to Top 20 schools, you're leaving out 3-5 schools that are in that group in any other year. Who is to say that #24 won't be #19 by the time you graduate? Law schools don't change significantly from year to year, but if U.S. News didn't change the rankings each year, it wouldn't be able to sell magazines.

Now that you've put the rankings in their rightful place, why would you choose a school in California if you want to practice in New York? It's all about location. Where do you want to live your life and practice law? If it's Los Angeles, pick Loyola over BU any day of the week. If it's New York, why go to Indiana-Bloomington instead of Cardozo just because U.S. News says so? Of course, you don't want to go to a 4th tier school when you could go to a top 20, but there are exceptions to this too, like scholarship money! But, in general, trust local lawyers and law firms over U.S. News every time.

Too many law school applicants make their decisions by the rankings. If you are going to make such a big decision based on what a magazine has to say, make sure you understand how law schools manipulate the rankings and why. Do your research.

There are so many flaws with ranking logic, and those statistical flaws are well documented on the web.

Let's also talk about the Tier 3 and Tier 4 Schools. I believe they should be regarded as "Regional Law Schools." Many of these schools have excellent reputations in their respective geographic regions and are at a disadvantage in the rankings since national reputation is a major factor relied upon by US News. Most lawyers practice law in a particular community for their entire careers. Attending law school in that community has distinct advantages that are not properly taken into account by the rankings. Are you going to be clerking for the Supreme Court as a graduate of a fourth tier school? No. But you can practice law, enjoy a respectable and rewarding career, and earn a good living by working hard for that living. Again, this involves developing realistic expectations of what a legal career is all about. When people tell me they only want to go to law school if they can go to Harvard, I tell them that they don't really want to go to law school.

My slogan is: "Don't be a snob; think about where you want a job."

How many schools should you apply to?

The answer to this question really depends on your professional goals, potential weaknesses in your application, and the strength of your experiences and how they are presented in your application. For example, if you have a problem in your application, like an arrest or academic probation, you should cast a wider net in order to find a school willing to take a chance on you. On the other side of the coin, if the city where you want to be only has three law schools, these suggestions do not apply to you.

A few years ago, I applied this rule of thumb:

- Apply to 2-4 schools where your LSAT is at the 25th percentile. ("Reach")
- Apply to 2 schools where your LSAT is at the 75th percentile. ("Safety")
- Apply to 3-5 schools where your LSAT is in between the 25th-75th percentiles of accepted applicants. ("Mid-Range")

Today, however, due to trends of people applying to more schools and admission decisions becoming more yield-conscious, I recommend that most applicants:

- Apply to 3-5 reach schools.
- Apply to 2-5 safety schools.
- Apply to 3-8 mid-range schools.

8 - 18 Schools

Why am I only counting LSAT? Because (for reasons discussed in Chapter 2), the GPA is too subjective. An upward grade trend can also make a difference. If your grades are in the 3.0-3.6 range, this rule of thumb will probably work for you if your applications are strong and they sell your strengths effectively. If your grades are below a 3.0, you should err on the side of applying to more mid-range and safety schools. Likewise, if your grades are strong you can be more liberal about the reach schools.

I do believe in maximizing your opportunities in deciding where to apply so you have real decisions to make in the spring. You will continue to learn more about the admission process and about law school in general during the year that you apply, and I want applicants to keep their options open to the extent possible. Therefore, the number of law schools you apply to will be largely constrained only by your budget for application and LSDAS report fees.

Full Time or Part Time?

Here are some things to think about in applying to part-time programs as part of your strategy for law school admission:

1. Is it a fully operating part-time program? If it's not a full section of students in the part-time program (around 100-130), the part-time option is probably intended for people who have significant work or family obligations. They may even attend part-time during the day or in a specially customized program for their situation. You may want to call the law school and find out more about the formality of the program.

2. How easy is it to transfer from part-time to full-time after the first year and still graduate in three years? If it's just a formality to transfer to full-time after taking two classes over the summer (whether on campus or as part of a study abroad program), this might be an attractive option.

3. Are you planning to try to transfer to another law school as a 2L? If so, you may be restricted to transferring only to schools that offer part-time programs and you'd probably remain a part time student throughout law school.

4. Consider your social and professional networking goals. Do you want to be surrounded by other people

who may be older, married, with families, and with professional careers under their belts? Or, do you want to be meeting other single people who have time to meet for Student Bar Association Thursday Night Keg parties? Socially, there can be a big difference between the demographics in part-time and full time programs, and the 1L year tends to be when people create lasting friendships.

If you are interested in part-time programs not as a "back door," but because you really will be working or taking care of a family in addition to attending law school, this is a fabulous option. When I began law school in 1996, I was a part-time evening student. I was busy pursuing a full time career in advertising and, while I wanted to go to law school, I wasn't ready to give up my full-time job. Here are some things I loved about being an evening student:

1. Nice people. My classmates were mostly older, had jobs and families, and had things in perspective. They were willing to work together and enjoy each other a little more than I think most of the younger, full-time day students were.
2. Faculty treated us more like adults and were generally more respectful toward the night students.
3. A little bit smaller section of students.

Here were some of the not so great things:

1. To take advantage of clubs and organizations (I was the evening program Student Bar Association

Representative, among my other involvements), you pretty much need to be available during the day.

2. Faculty and student services related offices are not usually available at night.

3. You're on a different curve than the day students, and they perceive the program as being "easier," since you can get on law review with a 3.5 and they need a 3.7 (this is not always the case, but is one of the sticky wickets about being a night student).

4. You need to take summer school to graduate in three years at most schools.

Each school's part-time program is different. For individual policies and circumstances, you need to talk to admissions officers at the school you're considering attending.

> How much of the fee waiver game is just that, a game to increase a school's selectivity numbers, and how much of it is because they really want to recruit you? "I was sure that Columbia offered me that fee waiver to pad their numbers, but I figured what the heck, why not, and boom, they accepted me. Michigan also offered me a fee waiver with a hand-written note from the director of admissions saying that they love getting students from my undergraduate college. I think that one was probably a genuine attempt at recruiting," said one of my clients, J.Z.
>
> However, another client got the fee waiver for Columbia and did not get in. (He is happily attending NYU, by the way).

Fee Waivers

Sometimes schools will offer application fee waivers. Obviously, there's no harm in taking a school up on this offer. Sometimes schools to do this to grab the attention of students they really want, and sometimes they do it simply to boost their application numbers to appear more selective in the rankings. Sometimes it's hard to know the difference.

Applying Early Decision and/or Early Notification

Erase any examples you have from undergrad of people who got into their college of choice simply by applying Early Decision. I have never seen this happen at the law school level. Binding Early Decision is another marketing ploy used by law schools to grab an additional level of commitment and gauge likelihood of attendance, and perhaps to snag a few people who will help bring up the numbers. If you are a mid-range applicant for a school and you apply Binding Early Decision, I bet Monopoly™ money that you'll be deferred to the regular admission cycle. If your numbers are in the top quartile of a school's student body, you might be sent a letter that says you're not admitted early decision and therefore not receiving scholarships, but, "Congratulations! You're admitted under our regular applicant pool." The good news is that, in that case, your acceptance of that offer probably isn't binding.

The only time I believe it's a good deal to apply early decision is if being admitted to the binding program means automatically getting a full scholarship to that school. However, even for schools that do have this arrangement, it's not the only way to obtain a full scholarship for that school, and you'd still have to be absolutely sure it's the school you'd want to attend, no matter what.

In the rare event that you are admitted under a binding Early Decision option, you may be wondering, "Exactly how binding is it?" LSAC lists obligations of the law schools and law school applicants in the admission process and one of the key obligations of a law school applicant is in regard to binding early decision programs. I strongly urge all law school applicants to read this one-page fact sheet available at lsac.org.

My personal advice is that you are entering a profession where your success will be based largely upon whether others regard you as being good for what you promise. It's a little early to start playing games with your reputation. Plus, you'll learn in law school that although it's not against the law to break a contract, there are certain liabilities and downsides for breaching a contract. While a law school won't send the police to cuff you, bring you to their campus, and make you pay the tuition, a law school very well might say "Nevermind" to your admission offer, as could the other school where you've submitted a deposit. Then where would you be? Would all of the trouble have been worth it?

PART III

AFTER APPLYING: THINGS TO CONSIDER

CHAPTER 12

WHAT DOES THE LAW SCHOOL DO WITH YOUR APPLICATION?

THE first thing a law school does when receiving your application is check it for completeness. Did you send the payment? Did you leave any required question responses blank? The second thing the school will do is make sure it has your LSAC Academic Summary report (the LSAC's calculation of your GPA, your GPA through the years of college, and how your GPA and LSAT numbers compare with others at your college) and your transcripts. The school will also make sure it receives the correct number of LORs from LSDAS. Once the school has all required materials, your file is deemed "Complete" and ready for review.

The first thing that happens during the review process is that you are assigned an "Index" number. Basically, each school has gone through a complicated statistical process to determine the numbers at which its graduates are most likely to succeed academically and pass the state's bar exam on the first try. Then, based on only the LSAC, GPA, and LSAT score (either average or highest score according to each school's policy), you are assigned a number. This number will mean absolutely nothing to you, and knowing this number will do you no good whatsoever.

The school will take that number and assign you to a pile. For example, if we pretend that a school has an index formula where all possible numbers are between 60 and 100, we can pretend the school divides each application into piles in this way:

85-100 Presumptive Admit
70-85   Committee
60-70   Presumptive Deny

Of course, each school does things a little differently, but this is the basic idea and it's applicable on some level at almost every law school (Yale being one notable exception). Once you are placed in a pile, the index number carries very little weight. In most cases, the Presumptive Admit files are reviewed by the director or dean of admissions (the title is different from school to school) and that individual decides either to admit the person or bump them down to the admission committee for further review. Reasons for the bump-down are usually pretty serious red flags, such as an arrest, incident of academic dishonesty, or something else in the file that smells fishy, like the person seeming troubled, arrogant, or inappropriate.

However, there's something else that has been happening with these files in the last year or two as of this printing. Obviously, these applicants assume they are applying to a safety school and that getting in is pretty much a sure thing. Some schools, however, are playing a game with these applicants and sending the very top applicants waitlist letters. They do this, of course, to make the applicant fight his way in and demonstrate that he would actually seriously consider attending the school. This is cruel, and you can thank U.S. News' reliance on acceptance rates for this practice.

Once the Presumptive Admit applicant is admitted, the director of admissions determines whether to offer the applicant a scholarship. In most cases, this news is shared in the offer of admission. Don't be surprised if you learn of your acceptance by phone or email because the next thing on the school's mind after admitting you is getting you to attend and that is where the recruiting phase really kicks into gear.

The Committee files are usually read by three faculty members of an admission committee. What is an admission committee? You've probably figured out it's nothing like the fictional one in Legally Blonde. The committee rarely meets to discuss a file, and is more likely to meet to discuss strategies, policies, and overall admission considerations. In most cases, an admission committee is made up of 8-10 faculty members who take piles of files, make comments and suggestions on the files, and then return them to the director of admission. "Law schools have an Admissions Committee composed primarily of faculty, but the committee typically reads less than half of the entire pool. In fact, in four of the schools where I have served, the faculty admissions committee has read only 10% or so of the entire pool." Says Dean Roboski.

Once three faculty members have voted on a file, a decision is made. You can see why these decisions take a long time. None of this happens instantaneously. This is also why two applicants whose files are complete on the same day will not necessarily receive their acceptance letters on the same day.

The director of admissions or assistant director will review the Presumptive Deny files. Any of those applicants who are impressive beyond the numbers (for reasons including maturity, work experience, life experience, diversity, etc.) will be bumped up to become a Committee file and will go through the same process outlined above.

> *"I have 3 questions when opening an application folder: 1) Can this applicant do well at my law school; 2) What qualities does this applicant have that I value in a student and future attorney; and 3) How does this applicant, who has the ability to excel at my law school and who has some or many of the qualities I value, compare to other applicants who are also academically able and who possess many of the qualities I value. This then leads into a discussion of rigor of courses, the mission of my law school, and values that we hold dear..."*
>
> —Charles Roboski, Assistant Dean of Admissions and Financial Aid at Michigan State University College of Law

CHAPTER 13

LAUNCHING YOUR CAMPAIGN TO GET IN

FOR the most part, this is your time to kick back and attempt to relax. However, there are some things you can do to help your cause without being viewed as annoying. These actions include:

1. Attending law school forums and recruiting events and introducing yourself to (but not stalking) the representatives of the schools where you applied.
2. Arranging official school visits through an admission office when it is convenient and accessible for you to do so.
3. Confirming (about 4-8 weeks after your file is submitted) that your file is complete and ready for review.

WAITLISTED? TAKE ACTION!

If you are placed on a waitlist, there is more you can do. To understand how to boost your chances of being admitted, you need to know what it means to be placed on a waitlist.

First, why were you waitlisted? Simple Answer: U.S. News & World Report Rankings. Schools are very concerned with their rankings and an easy way for them to control things from an admission standpoint are (a) watching the LSAT/GPA for admitted students; and (b) keeping acceptance rates low. What this means is that if you are at or below a school's median LSAT and GPA, it may waitlist you and make you fight your way in to make sure that you are highly likely to attend the school. In addition, a recent, annoying trend is for law schools to waitlist people with numbers above the 75th percentile LSAT and GPA range because the school doesn't believe you would actually attend and doesn't want to waste a precious acceptance letter on you. This is what is called "protecting the yield."

How do you demonstrate that your attendance is likely? Here are some ways:

1. Visit the law school. Schedule a visit through the admissions office and ask to sit in on a class and go on a tour. You may even have the opportunity to meet with someone in the admissions office. This shows your interest and likelihood to attend a school in the geographic region.

2. Follow up with a thank-you letter reiterating your interest in the school based on what you learned during your visit. Be specific!

3. If you can't visit, write a letter with an update about what you've done since submitting your application.

4. Write a letter stating the reasons for your specific interest in that law school and highlight things from your background that tie into those interests.

5. Send an additional Letter of Recommendation if it is allowed.

6. Keep the lines of communication open. Always tell

the school's representative when he or she can expect to hear from you next. ("I plan to call your office at the end of April once the first deposit deadline has passed...")

How Law Schools Evaluate Waitlists

A client asked me the following question about how law schools evaluate the waitlist when deciding whom to admit:

"I was wondering if you could give me a little more insight about how wait lists usually work. Is there a weighted order in which applicants are ranked and then applicants are taken off according to that? Is the ranking based on their admissions index number or the order in which they received apps? Would retaking the LSAT in June and getting a higher score give them more of a reason to take an applicant off the waiting list?"

As a director of admission for a law school, I looked at my waitlist for a combination of the following:

1. Likelihood of attendance if offered admission.
2. Numbers. Keeping an eye on how medians, 25th and 75th percentiles were shaping up given which admitted applicants submitted deposits, I wanted to make sure adding new folks to the mix would not detrimentally alter my numbers.
3. Diversity. Evaluating the diversity, including gender balance, of admitted applicants who submitted deposits, I wanted to see whether the class would be lacking diverse students and whether any applicants who passed #1 and #2 (above) would help round out the class in this respect.

I didn't have time to make phone calls going down the list. I wanted to make one call to an applicant who would be thrilled to hear from me and who would commit to my school on the spot.

This is why Letters of Continued Interest are so important. This is why likeability is a factor. Whose day do I want to make? That's what I would think about.

Now, not every school uses its waitlist in the same way, and not every school uses its waitlist the same way from year to year or week to week. Some do place people in quartiles or priority lists. Others use numbers only or residents first or perhaps even consider diversity factors depending on how it seems the class is shaping up so far. You can't predict what will happen, and nothing I tell you will change that.

> One of my clients was waitlisted at the part time program for her dream school, got pulled in from the wait list, then talked her way into the full time program before Orientation even began. No one ever knew that's how she got there. But if her strategy had been sitting and hoping and praying, it never would have happened. "If you are willing to stand up for yourself and show a school why you belong there, with concrete evidence, you can make things happen that otherwise wouldn't." She said.

The key thing to keep in mind is that, yes, people get into their dream schools off the waitlist. Absolutely. So, if it's important to you, pursue it. If you're staying on the waitlist just to get another acceptance letter in your portfolio, perhaps consider a polite bowing out in favor of that applicant who would be thrilled at the acceptance. (Just because the law schools play games doesn't mean you have to.)

Lastly, I have seen people improve on the June LSAT and be admitted off a waitlist as a result. Yes. I had a client with a 165 waitlisted at Northwestern. He came back with a 170 on the June LSAT and was admitted.

One word of caution: Please be polite to people who work at law schools. Most of them are not paid well, they are overworked, trying to do a good job, but mistakes do happen. Be professional in all of your dealings; remember that if you act like a jerk (or spoiled brat) these people have the power to walk right into the Dean of Admissions and share a story about the unkind applicant. Reports like this will not help you be selected from the waitlist, and will probably expedite your rejection letter. It is an important lesson for aspiring lawyers to treat secretaries and assistants very, very well.

Multiple Deposits

By June of each year, law schools will be able to see where you've submitted seat deposits. If a school sees that you have multiple deposits, the school has the right to enforce any policy it has in regard to withdrawing offers of admission. Therefore, before sending deposits to more than one school, you should find out each school's policy in this regard. Some schools may retain the right to cancel their offer of admission, and other schools may allow multiple deposits. Don't be caught off guard. The consequences could be detrimental.

CHAPTER 14

TAKING TIME OFF
BEFORE LAW SCHOOL

DECIDING between going straight into law school from college and taking time off before law school is not a question of one option being better than the other. People from both tracks are admitted to law school. The question is what would you do with this time off? Many people go to law firms as paralegals, legal assistants, and file clerks. They think they will gain some significant insight into the legal profession and get an attorney or two to tell a law school how they brilliantly saved a case for the firm. Yeah, ummm, not going to happen. You're really just going to have a boring year typing for long hours while busy lawyers bark at you. You'll also be applying to law school while enduring those long hours. After all that, you'll have only spent three months at the firm by the time you apply. How outstanding a letter of recommendation do you think you're going to get?

Better ideas? Yes. Find your passion! Find something that will set you apart and help you find a niche. It can be anything from skydiving instruction to teaching the viola. The key is to explore one of your passions. Plus, it's probably one of the last times in your life that you can spend your day doing something really fun, something you enjoy, whether or not it's related to the law. It's also probably the last time you'll be able to get away with only making $25,000 per year.

I advocate taking the time off to perform significant community service work (Peace Corps, Americorps/Teach for America), to get good grades in a graduate program for those people whose undergraduate grades are embarrassing, or to demonstrate growth and maturity if there are things in people's backgrounds that will be worrisome to law schools (multiple drug related incidents, etc.). However, another reason might be if you are over-committed during your senior year of college and cannot bring your grades up while studying for the LSAT and applying to law school. This decision requires some honest introspection and self-evaluation.

> If you are considering taking a job in a law firm to explore whether practicing law is the right profession for you, then do it for a year without applying to law school that same year. In other words, plan to work for two years. Take a year to explore the profession. Then once you know what it's all about you can spend your second year on the job applying to law school. It's very difficult to learn a job and do it well at the same time that you're applying to law school. Plus, you'll garner LORs that are more meaningful by working for a more significant amount of time.

One of my former clients adds a really vital perspective to this decision:

I took 4 years off and I most certainly appreciate the time I took off. You don't have to be poor for a few years after college. You can go into investment banking (if it still exists) or work for

Boeing or Microsoft or whatever that still pays. Working allows you to really weigh the pros and cons of going back to school and getting that JD degree. Perhaps this advice isn't so adequate for those students who really know that they want to be a lawyer, but how many 22 year-olds really have such a concrete plan for the future?

I don't think you necessarily need to try hard to find your passion or to save the world. Just see where things take you and maybe you'll love the field you chose, or maybe you will find your true passion is law. But I wouldn't say you really need to try too hard to find your passion. Let it happen.

Another benefit to my work experience was that it was easier to find a job for the summer after my 1L year. I was able to get a summer associate position at a big firm because of my significant work experience in the IT industry.

Another advantage to waiting might be if news agencies are reporting significantly increased applications to law school. If you can be flexible about waiting for a few years, it might increase your chances of getting into a reach school.

CHAPTER 15

HIRING A LAW SCHOOL ADMISSION CONSULTANT

A good consultant gives you an added layer of guidance and confidence. However, if you are only applying to one or two schools, your LSAT and undergraduate GPA is in line with what they are looking for, and there are no problem areas in your application, you probably do not need a consultant.

Law school applicants who benefit the most from working with a consultant usually have a weakness in their application, such as a low grade point average, poor LSAT score, an arrest, or have been out of school for a significant amount of time. In today's reality of getting into school, they truly need the help of a good consultant.

You will benefit from working with a law school admission consultant if:

(a) You are out of college and/or do not have access to a helpful and knowledgeable pre law adviser.
(b) You feel overwhelmed by the process of applying to law school.
(c) You work better when you are held accountable to someone.

(d) You would like to get your parents, spouse, or significant other out of the process and have access to an objective and knowledgeable third party to answer your questions and assist you in making the right decisions for yourself.

(e) You don't know where to start and feel like you're spinning your wheels.

(f) You have a tendency to procrastinate.

(g) You are re-applying to law school.

(h) You simply want the best of everything and to arm yourself with every possible advantage in this competitive process.

IMPORTANT CONSIDERATIONS IN HIRING A LAW SCHOOL ADMISSION CONSULTANT

1. Is the consultant a law school specialist? Does he also help people apply to other graduate and undergraduate programs? What is his specific experience with law school admissions? Does he also help people apply to MBA programs? Is he giving career advice to recent grads? Doing a book tour? Practicing law? How high up will you be on the priority list of this very busy person?

2. Will you be working directly with this person or with her employees? Does she have someone else do editing? Who will actually be picking up the phone and giving you advice?

3. Does the consultant specialize in helping people who are applying to the caliber of schools you hope to attend? Will the consultant place the same importance

on each piece of your application that they will on the applicant applying to Harvard?

4. How much time does the consultant have to work with you? Is the fee based on hours or the number of schools you will be applying to, or is it for unlimited advice based on your personal needs and issues?

5. Do you need to make an appointment or do you feel free to call and have an open discussion whenever you're feeling overwhelmed, confused, or down?

6. How fast will your emails and phone messages be answered? How quickly will your essay drafts be turned around?

7. Is the person willing to give you references of current and former clients with goals, credentials, and a geographic region similar to yours? Does the consultant have testimonials from former clients?

8. Why did the consultant choose to be a law school admission consultant? Did the person fail the bar exam or have trouble finding employment and resort to consulting? What motivates her and on what experience does she base her expertise? Has she actually made law school admission decisions?

9. What kind of record of accomplishment does the consultant have with helping people get into schools with test results at or below the 25th percentile?

10. Is consulting his full-time job or is he practicing law and using this to supplement his income?

Applying to law school is stressful and overwhelming, but it doesn't need to be. With the right expert and coach by your side, you will feel supported and confident.

Utilizing the Assistance of a College Pre-Law Advisor

Most undergraduate schools offer a pre law advisor for its students. Some of these advisors are attorneys and some are not. For some, pre-law advising is a full time job, and for others it is not. The only way to gauge how helpful your school's advisor will be in your process is to arrange a meeting with the advisor. One pre-law advisor at a large public university told me, "Some of my colleagues barely know how many times a year the LSAT is offered and students will get very little benefit working with their school's government professor who gets an extra $1,000 to have the title of pre-law advisor." However, a good advisor can be an incredibly valuable asset to an applicant, especially if that person has some experience and training in the law school admissions process in addition to being a law school graduate.

CHAPTER 16

WHAT I WISH I'D KNOWN BEFORE APPLYING TO LAW SCHOOL

THIS chapter is intended to be read for different purposes at different times in the admission cycle. It's probably a good thing to read when you're deciding whether law school is right for you. It's equally good to read when you're waiting you're your decisions and just hoping to distract yourself from the agony of not knowing while still thinking about the greater goal. It's especially important to read right before you start law school when you think about the kind of law student you hope to be.

There are more aspects to this than just the kind of student you hope to be in the classroom. During my law school orientation, the Vice Dean told us that there was nothing more important in building a legal career than our reputations. He urged us to remember this in our dealings with each other. He also made the joke "Look to the right, look to the left" but instead of saying one in three of us would fail out, he told us that one in three would be divorced by graduation. Both warnings proved true.

In law school, you decide whether you will be a good friend or whether you will only look out for yourself. You decide who is worth sharing notes with and who can be trusted to help you when you have the flu and desperately need chicken soup. You watch people in the most casual of circumstances and decide whether that person is too nervous to ever refer a case to or whether someone's ego will make you cringe when you meet five years later in a courtroom.

Because this is such an important time in the building of your career, I compiled some advice and food for thought from friends, former colleagues, law school administrators, and former clients for their insights about things they wish they'd known before applying to law school.

DONALD WEST, JR.
PRESIDENT, AXIS LAW GROUP, P.L., ATLANTA, GA
J.D., UNIVERSITY OF MIAMI SCHOOL OF LAW

I wish I'd had a better understanding of the business principles of legal practice. In most law schools, excellent instruction is provided on legal reasoning, legal theory, research, and writing. However, in many instances we are acquiring these skills to generate an income to support our families and ourselves. Most law schools fall short of preparing students to handle the business behind the practice of law. It is important for all of us as legal practitioners to also be astute businessmen and women, as it is a foundational element to our professional craft.

I also wish I'd understood the value of networking. In a way, your law school becomes a part of your extended family. I say this because once you graduate with your Juris Doctor degree you are essentially married to that particular institution. No matter what your experience or opinion of the place, your alma mater is a name you cannot escape. The individuals that attend law school with you will be your life-long partners as you progress from a common starting point. Understanding the basic principles of professional networking, and utilizing the knowledge while on your law school campus, will reap a lifetime of rewards and provide you with many genuinely enhancing relationships.

Many people say, "You should go to law school where you intend to practice law." I believe that one of the reasons that this is mentioned is because of the network you build in your local community in addition to the benefits of learning the laws of the local jurisdiction in your classes. The American Bar Association and your local bar association can also be career long partners for your professional growth and development. Active participation will allow the astute networker to build meaningful national and local contacts to assist him through his career's numerous twists and turns.

Lastly, I wish I'd had a greater appreciation for academic excellence. Grades are an important part of the law school process. I knew this fact going in, but I could not articulate why they were important. During my first year in law school I had the privilege of meeting an attorney, Mary Ann Connors, who shared this insight. "Law students with superior academic records correlate into faster producing workers on the job. The skills they mastered in keeping up with their classroom assignments amidst all of life's challenges are the same skills a law firm needs from its associates." In addition to the great benefits of post-graduation employment, many law firms will ask to see your law transcripts five, ten, and even fifteen years after you have graduated.

SHIRLEY LI
3L, BOSTON COLLEGE LAW SCHOOL

I wish I'd concentrated less on attending a Top 14 School and realized that other schools could also lead to higher paying jobs. I attended an Ivy-league university for undergrad. After graduation, I took a year off to be a paralegal at a top-tier NY firm, where I was surrounded by lawyers who got their JDs from Harvard, Columbia, Yale, and Georgetown. I knew the value of a name brand law school and pretty soon it was ingrained in my mind that if I went to any law school other than the T-14, I would not be getting a $160K per year job.

I took the LSAT twice, got the same miserable score both times, and cancelled a third time. I felt dejected. Despite my decent undergrad GPA, I knew that I would not be getting into a T-14 school no matter how hard I tried. The best schools I was accepted into were Boston College Law School and then off the waitlist at another school that was in the middle of nowhere and wouldn't translate well if I wanted to go back to New York.

I visited BCLS and honestly, at the time I didn't know the difference between BC and BU. During Admit Day, I fell in love with the people there. Everyone I met was friendly and seemed very genuine. I knew they had a very strong reputation in Boston and that it would be very doable for me to transfer back to New York from Boston. I decided to go. I remained extremely worried that I would be racking up lots of debt with no payoff. Everyone also told me that since I wasn't going to a top tier school, I would need to be at the top of my class to compete with the Harvard kids.

This past summer, I interned for a federal district court judge in the Massachusetts District Court. I finished pretty well in my class (nowhere excellent, but decent). I wrote onto a journal. I recruited in both New York and Boston. At the end of September, I had offers from two of my top choices, both of which are nationally ranked in the top 15 by Vault and ranked in AmLaw's A-List as well as the AmLaw 100. Both are firms I thought I would NEVER get into because I went to BCLS and because, frankly, most of the people going to these firms ARE from the T-14. Much of where you end up is what you put in.

I know classmates who were bottom 50th percentile who had strong work experience that helped them get big law jobs. Others just did really well in law school, but they came in with weaker undergrad degrees. It all depends on what you have to offer. Yes, my Ivy League undergrad helped. My internship with the judge helped. If you are determined to do well, you will. I know friends who are at USC and Georgetown, much higher ranked schools than BC, who cannot get a job because they performed poorly in law school.

One last thing I wish I'd known: your LSAT is not indicative of how you will do in law school. Most of my friends on law review who scored in the top 10% of the class had LSAT scores below the 25th percentile for entering students at our school. Law school is about having a good work ethic and discipline. If you are going to law school because you don't know what else to do, you should probably think about it long and hard. However, if you think the law is something that will challenge you and you know that you're going to put in the time and effort, it's a good option. No matter where you go, you will have to do well.

SARA YOOD
1L, FORDHAM LAW SCHOOL

Law school is really, really hard. I am so glad that I waited for five years between undergrad and graduate school. It has given me a maturity that I don't see in many of my classmates that has been extremely beneficial in dealing with the rigors of 1L year. If a professor asks me a question, I am not afraid to say "I don't know." That's why I'm in the class in the first place - to learn. Being in a dead-end job in the real world taught me the value of the education I am getting. Knowing what it's like to be undervalued gives me the motivation every day to work hard and participate in all of the amazing things that happen at school.

Going to law school doesn't mean losing your soul. I am involved in many of the same things in law school that have always been my passions (singing, reproductive justice, politics) while exploring new areas of service. Law schools have tons of programs you can get involved in to donate your time, raise awareness of legal issues, and help real people. Even if you want to become a lawyer at a big law firm, you can still work with these worthy organizations, and keep your soul while you're at it.

LAURIE MORGAN
JUNIOR PARTNER AT LEWIS, MARENSTEIN, WICKE & SHERWIN,
WOODLAND HILLS, CA
J.D., SANTA CLARA UNIVERSITY SCHOOL OF LAW

If you plan to stay in the same location where you're going to law school, it pays to be nice to EVERYONE. You never know who you'll run into down the line in your practice who can help or hurt you.

Jenn Duffy
Partner, Fell Marking LLP, Santa Barbara, CA
J.D., University of San Francisco School of Law

"It isn't about the money. You have to love helping people, or the law, or -- preferably -- both. The money will come, but if you are in it for the money, you will not have a happy life. It takes a very long time to pay off student loans."

Randee Breiter
Former Associate Director of Career Planning at the University of Miami School of Law, FL
J.D. University of Miami School of Law

I think it is important that students realize that all (well, most) students who go to law school are smart. No one goes to law school who doesn't think they are bright. Most expect to be at the top of their class, yet most end up somewhere in the middle. There are jobs for everyone, just different types of jobs with different salaries. This is another reason to be careful about your debt load.

Jeremiah Harvey
2L, UC Davis School of Law

1. DON'T DATE ANYONE IN LAW SCHOOL.
2. Get a (preferably law) roommate and pick carefully. Roommates become your best friend and best resource (you are supposed to be the same).
3. The people you meet in law school you will know for the rest of your life: A) get to know them; B) don't be the person no one likes; C) get and give help whenever you can.
4. The gym is your friend. Sitting behind a desk 13 hours per day with food and coffee can mess with

your body. Take care of it and enjoy the time away from your desk.

5. No matter what you do in the law chant: "attention to detail, attention to detail, attention to detail."

6. Law school exams are based on one test 3-9 hours long typing. Those who can type well don't have to worry about their typing and thus have an advantage. Learn to type well before you take your first final.

AMANDA ELLIS
FOUNDER AND ATTORNEY SEARCH CONSULTANT,
AMANDA ELLIS LEGAL SEARCH, DALLAS, TX
J.D., UNIVERSITY OF TEXAS SCHOOL OF LAW

Law school grades are more important than ever. At least 90% of the firms I work with inquire about lateral candidates' law school grades. I won't get into a discussion here on whether law school grades are more important than the rank of the law school, but I can tell you that the majority of the firms I work with scrutinize a lateral candidate's grades more closely than the rank of the candidate's law school. In the past month, I've seen three large firms move forward with candidates who graduated in the top 5% from a Tier 4 law school; this illustrates that a candidate can do well at a lower tier school and still land in a large firm. The one caveat I would emphasize is that a large firm typically only hires candidates from Tier 4 law schools within the firm's legal market. For example, a graduate of a Tier 4 school in Texas will have a harder time finding a job outside of Texas even if he or she finished in the top 5% whereas large Texas firms are likely to consider the candidate.

Certain legal markets give greater weight to grades than others. Based on my experience placing lateral attorneys in multiple states, Texas firms have one of the most stringent grading scales. The major firms in Texas base their hiring criteria on the U.S. News rankings. Generally, a candidate from a Top 15 law school must finish in the top 40-50% in order to qualify as a potential hire for large Texas firms. Candidates from other Tier 1 schools typically must finish in the top 15-25% and candidates from Tier 2 schools must finish in the top 10-15% in order to qualify. Candidates from Tier 3 and Tier 4 schools typically must finish in the Top 5-10% in order to meet the hiring standards for large firms in Texas (though certain Tier 4 schools are favored over others). I've worked with firms in other legal markets that are not this strict; for example, the cutoff for Tier 1 schools is the top 50% in some markets.

CHAPTER 17

DECIDING WHERE TO ATTEND

What's Important in a Law School

JOBS. It's that simple. You must consider which school will give you the most access to jobs. Some considerations:

1. Talk to someone in the Career Services office at the law school. Ask for statistics. Who interviews on campus and who is interviewed. Do recruiters go only after the Top 10 percent? How many people are hired through On-Campus Interviews (OCI)? What are other ways that the office supports students, whether or not they are selected for OCI?

2. Talk to recent graduates about their experiences finding employment.

3. Call law firms in the geographic location where you hope to practice law. Ask where they recruit and whom they hire.

One of my former clients who is currently attending NYU Law School advocates strongly for location as the primary factor in choosing a law school. "You have no idea how many networking opportunities I have by being in New York, and also there are so many things you can do in law school, term time internships, job interviews without traveling, many symposiums and guest lectures at surrounding law schools, student groups being able to work together with local NGOs like Housing Works," he said.

A REALISTIC LOOK AT TAKING ON DEBT

If you are going to law school in order to make gobs of money right out of the starting gate, you're making a huge mistake. One of attorney friends said it best when he told me over a fancy, firm-expensed dinner, "We're really just the highest paid blue-collar workers." He's right in the respect that this is real work. It's demanding. The hours are long. There is potential for a lot of money if you work like a dog, but even if you work like a dog, you'll be doing well just by making $100,000 each year. You cannot expect to be making that immediately upon graduation from law school.

As of this printing, the economy is in terrible condition. Big firms where recent law school graduates make the most money are firing attorneys and revoking offers they've already made to soon-to-be law school graduates. This is the best possible fact I could provide in order to urge you not to place your entire bet on a top 10 law school in exchange for taking on $200,000 in debt. Now more than ever, the benefits of taking a full scholarship and having the luxury of making $60,000 right out of school are apparent.

Does going to a lesser-ranked law school preclude you from some career options? Yes. You probably won't be clerking for the Supreme Court and you may not be seriously considered for a career in academia. But I can list many examples of people who graduate without honors from regional law schools who may start out at $60,000 per year, then are promoted within a year or two to making $85,000, then a couple years after that they surpass $100,000, and after 7-10 years in practice make about $150,000 per year. Will you be buying yachts at this rate? No. Will you be able to support your family? Yes, if you're smart and if you don't take on a crazy amount of debt.

The important thing is to keep an open mind about all of your options and to analyze them carefully. Talk to recent law school graduates, attorneys at firms of all sizes, and legal recruiters. Know what you are getting yourself into before it's too late.

> A recent trend at top 15 schools is to invite applicants to apply for scholarships. I believe the reason for this is the new trend where certain schools (Berkeley) offer to match any scholarship offer by a top 15 school. Schools know that applicants use scholarship letters to negotiate with other schools about obtaining additional scholarships, and no school wants to be "used" in this respect. Therefore, by making you write an essay to be considered for the scholarship, the school is making you work a little harder for it by showing you would actually be very likely to accept the offer.

Scholarships

One of the most important decisions you can make is whether to accept a scholarship to a lower ranked school versus paying full price and going into debt to attend a more highly ranked school. When evaluating scholarship offers, there are some important questions you should ask:

1. What are the terms of renewability?
2. What is the likelihood of meeting those terms? It's a much better scholarship offer if all you need to do is remain a student "in good standing" as opposed to having to maintain a 3.25 GPA or be ranked in the top 25 percent of your class.
3. Does the scholarship convert to a loan if you transfer after your first year?
4. What is the likelihood of an increased scholarship after your first year if you finish in the top 10 percent or 20 percent of the class?

It's also important to consider the living expenses and any residency thresholds you might be able to meet by signing a lease in-state and/or spending a certain amount of time in the state.

Another big topic about scholarships is negotiating offers between schools. It's no secret that this practice occurs. Berkeley now even offers to match scholarships given by any top 14 law school (as of this printing). The first question is usually, "What are the downsides of asking a school to increase a scholarship offer?" If you approach the issue politely and without a sense of entitlement, and seem sincerely interested in attending the school as opposed to amassing offers for your scrapbook or for the purpose of showing them to other schools, then there's not a lot of downside.

A law school is more likely to increase its scholarship offer if you were offered more money by a school considered a competitor. Don't expect the University of Iowa and University of Santa Clara to fight over you. It's not going to happen. However, University of San Francisco might compete with University of

Santa Clara and the University of Illinois might compete with the University of Iowa. These are obviously just examples for the purpose of showing what I mean by "competition." It has to do with geography and ranking, and of course depends upon how badly a school really wants you. Don't assume a school can't live without you; be polite and courteous and likeable in all of your dealings with employees and faculty members. Act like a professional, but one who is passionate about the possibility of contributing to and attending the school.

One of my clients was offered scholarships to both Rutgers and Seton Hall and said he liked Seton Hall but the cost was still a lot more than Rutgers. I advised him to call the admission office at Seton Hall to see if anything could be done. A week later, his scholarship was increased enough to make the two schools cost exactly the same.

When approaching a school about scholarship terms, try to be personal about it. Don't send an e-mail to the generic admission office address and expect a prompt response. Contact a real person such as someone who signed your scholarship letter or someone with whom you've interacted at a recruiting event or during a campus visit. Ask about the best way to follow up considering the school's procedure for awarding scholarships.

CHAPTER 18

WHAT TO DO THE SUMMER BEFORE LAW SCHOOL

YOU are already admitted to law school. This is not a summer that you need for resume building purposes; you have three years in law school to build a resume relevant to the legal profession. This is your last summer to really do what you love. Whether it's volunteering, traveling, or reading mystery novels, I urge you to do anything unrelated to law that you enjoy. You'll have law for the rest of your life, and I promise that you won't have time for pleasure reading for a while. Do what you love, be with the people you love, and enjoy every precious moment.

Many of my clients ask about the commercial prep courses for law school, where they probably teach you the IRAC method for briefing cases and writing exams. Unless you got into law school by the skin of your teeth and have no history of academic success, you really don't need these programs. I suppose there is value in feeling more confident on the first day of law school, even if there is no real basis for the confidence. However, part of succeeding in law school is figuring out what works for you and learning in a style that suits you. You're just going to have to dive in and try it. In a few months you'll wish you'd saved the course registration fee for a few extra beers on Friday nights after class.

There are a few types of prospective law students whom I believe might benefit from Law Preview or an equivalent course. If you feel out of practice with studying techniques, you may benefit from getting your head in the game a little early. If you suffer from a general lack of confidence and feel as though everyone else is smarter and more deserving in every situation, you might benefit from becoming a little more acquainted with your surroundings in order to increase your comfort level on your first day of law school. I doubt, however, that there is any difference in academic performance between those who participate in these courses and those who spend that week reading chic lit by the pool.

CHAPTER 19

TRANSFERRING

YOU should never select a law school with the intention of transferring after your first year; doing so will only set you up for disappointment and you will find yourself quite disgruntled as a 2L and 3L should transferring not work out for you. However, it's good to know that if you finish your 1L year with good grades, you can transfer into some amazing schools. Why does this work? Because schools don't have to report your LSAT and GPA to the ABA, so it doesn't count in rankings. This is the best "back door" into a school that is better than your numbers.

Some examples? I've helped clients transfer from Golden Gate to William and Mary, from Catholic to Georgetown, from George Mason to Northwestern, and from Touro to Cardozo. What is the secret? Good grades during your first year of law school. It's that simple.

What are the downsides?

1. Moving at a moment's notice.
2. Picking up and starting over in a new social and academic environment.
3. Finding yourself ineligible for On Campus Interviews and membership on the law review at the school you hope to attend.

4. It's unpredictable; schools do not report where they accept transfers from, what they seek in terms of class ranking, or how many transfer applications they receive each year.

Once you know your options, you can decide whether the downsides outweigh the upsides. The only thing to be careful about is your current law school's policy on students with transfer applications under consideration at other schools. Loyola Law School recently made headlines when it prohibited any of its 1Ls with outstanding transfer applications from participating in On Campus Interviews; this may be the beginning of a trend.

Randee Breiter, who spent 14 years as the Assistant Director of Career Planning and Placement at the University of Miami School of Law, told me:

When considering transferring to a "better" school, look at your reasons. If you are transferring because you want to be in academia, or you want to work in the city the new school is in then great. But if your dream job is in the city your current school is in and you are moving to another town, be careful. Chances are that firm hires from the top of the class at your current school and you will be a good candidate, and by transferring you may actually be hurting your chances. I had a UM student transfer to NYU and then apply for a job at a big law firm in Miami. The firm didn't interview him at NYU but, had he stayed at UM, he would definitely have gotten an interview.

CHAPTER 20

PARTING WORDS

LAW school is an adventure and the most stressful, time consuming part of any adventure is planning for it. The application process is daunting, overwhelming, and stressful. You will find a lot of cross-messages and inconsistent information on the Internet. Before you drive yourself crazy, consider the source of the information. Just as you wouldn't take relationship advice from a friend who has never been in a productive and healthy relationship, avoid listening too much to those who are not incredibly knowledgeable about the subject matter.

As hard as it will be, try to keep things in perspective. Work hard to attain your goals, but remember that the world will not end if you are rejected from your first choice law school. There is something to be said for being a bigger fish in a smaller pond. Realize that you can enjoy a fine career as a graduate of any ABA law school just like there are plenty of failures who graduate from top schools. The initiative you take in making yourself marketable is what will make the difference in building your path to success.

ABOUT THE AUTHOR

A NN K. Levine is a law school admission consultant and the owner of www.LawSchoolExpert.com. Since 2004, Ann has assisted more than 1,000 law school applicants through the admission process. Almost 100,000 people read her pre-law advice blog in 2008.

After graduating *magna cum laude* from the University of Miami School of Law, she served as Director of Student Services at the University of Denver College of Law, as Director of Admissions for California Western School of Law and Loyola Law School in Los Angeles. She (briefly) practiced law in Colorado and California before opening Law School Expert.

Ann lives in Santa Barbara, California with her husband (an attorney) and their two daughters. She also serves as Regional Board Chair for the Anti-Defamation League and attempts to run 10k races, knit, shop with friends, and watch Top Chef, 24, Ugly Betty, and American Idol in her spare time.

You can follow Ann on Twitter @annlevine and become a fan of "The Law School Admission Game" on Facebook.

INDEX